PICK
A HORSE

PICK A HORSE

THE POWER TO CHOOSE YOU

NOELLE RANDALL

Copyright © 2024 by Noelle Randall

All rights reserved. In accordance with the U.S. Copyright Act of 1976, the scanning, uploading, and electronic sharing of any part of this book without the permission of the publisher constitute unlawful piracy and theft of the author's intellectual property. If you would like to use material from the book (other than for review purposes), prior written permission must be obtained by contacting the publisher at books@waltonpublishinghouse.com. Reviewers may quote brief passages in reviews.

Walton Publishing House
Weston, Florida
www.waltonpublishinghouse.com
Printed in the United States of America

The advice found within may not be suitable for every individual. This work is purchased with the understanding that neither the author nor the publisher are held responsible for any results. Neither author nor publisher assumes responsibility for errors, omissions, or contrary interpretations of the subject matter herein. Any perceived disparagement of an individual or organization is a misinterpretation.

Brand and product names mentioned are trademarks that belong solely to their respective owners.
Library of Congress Cataloging-in-Publication Data under ISBN: 978-1-953993-88-5

Dedication

THIS BOOK IS affectionately dedicated to the mentors who have illuminated my path. Throughout my journey, I've been fortunate to encounter incredible mentors, especially during times when I needed guidance the most.

My heartfelt thanks go to Lisa Sasevich, Lisa Cherney, and Jason Waldrop for their unwavering support. I also extend my gratitude to my virtual mentors, Tony Robbins, Bob Proctor, Esther Hicks, Mel Robbins, Eric Thomas (ET the Hip Hop Preacher), Eddie Pinero, and Steven Bartlett. Your teachings, through words and writings, have been my beacon of light especially in those times of need.

To each and every one of you, this book is a tribute. You have each, in your unique way, been a source of inspiration in my life.

Prologue

> **"Our best thoughts come from others."**
>
> Ralph Waldo Emerson

I STAND ON THE shoulders of giants—remarkable mentors, visionary leaders, and transformative authors have all played a part in molding me. Among my most influential teachers are those I have never had the opportunity to meet in person. Those who have mastered their crafts and achieved remarkable feats inspire me deeply. Observing people from diverse backgrounds who challenge and offer fundamental life principles to the world has been enlightening. *The Four Agreements: A Practical Guide to Personal Freedom* by Don Miguel Ruiz has been a significant influence, teaching me the power of using words wisely. It's shown me the importance of not making assumptions, not taking things personally, and always doing my best.

Striving for my personal best has been a key factor in shaping who I am today.

I wrote this book to share my authentic journey without oversimplifying or invalidating others' experiences. The insights I offer here are the pillars of my own success—making bold choices, committing fully to a direction, and trusting in my ability to make optimal decisions. It is not my intention to tell you what to do or how to do it. Rather, my goal is to encourage you to aim for your highest potential and to cultivate the best version of yourself. I hope you find solace in your personal belief system and discover that by questioning and possibly moving beyond some of these beliefs, you can embark on a new chapter in your life.

CONTENTS

Dedication v
Prologue vii
Introduction xi

Chapter 1   You Have the Power to Choose 1
Chapter 2   Survival of the Fittest: From Employee to
                Business Owner 18
Chapter 3   You Can't Hide 41
Chapter 4   Pick Your Horse and Rein It In 59
Chapter 5   Choose To Be Great 84
Chapter 6   What Will It Take to Achieve Your
                Success? 108
Chapter 7   Who's Coming With You? 130
Chapter 8   What's Your Story? 166
Chapter 9   What If You Fail? 176
Chapter 10 Don't Chase It! Get in the Flow of
                Wealth 198
Chapter 11 Embrace the Process and Ride It! 216

References 225
Acknowledgments 231
About the Author 233
Stay Connected 236
Other books by Noelle 237

Introduction

WELCOME TO YOUR new journey towards wealth and success!

When my publisher asked what I would call my book, I immediately remembered the words that altered the course of my life. I was once a very "scattered" entrepreneur who dabbled in a variety of enterprises without fully committing to any of them. When I told my then-mentor about my various efforts, she gently said, "Pick a horse and ride it!" That seemingly simple counsel pushed me to pursue my real estate passion, setting me on a road that has made me millions of dollars.

This book is filled with my insights and the strategies I use to sharpen my business acumen and build my credibility in the business community. I hope that you will not only take in the material but also be motivated to put the principles into practice as soon as you finish read-

PICK A HORSE

ing. The wisest choice I ever made was to start taking action. After all the blood, sweat, and tears, I can say with confidence that hard work and persistence pay off.

I am now passing the baton to you with the same loving energy that my mentor bestowed upon me. It's time for you to pick a horse and ride it! Why? Because you have the power to choose you!

To your success,
Noelle

CHAPTER ONE

You Have the Power to Choose

I<small>N THE WINTER</small> of 2008, I found myself lying naked on the cold, wet tile, crying uncontrollably. The pang of failure shot deep within my gut, pulling me to the floor. I was losing my home and everything I had fought so hard for. Blaring like loud sirens, I replayed the voices of the harassing creditor calls and payday loan lenders. *I had reached my breaking point.* For months, there were non-stop threatening debt collector letters and warnings about upcoming bank foreclosures. I recall thinking to myself; *it shouldn't be this difficult to provide money and freedom for my family.* It felt as if I was being punished for deciding to break away from the regular rut and routine that so many had fallen victim to. I was fighting

PICK A HORSE

hard against the matrix—where people worked jobs they hated, looked forward to the ever-so-short weekend, and like clockwork would complain on Monday that it was too damn short! The matrix of mediocrity.

My life was spinning out of control. I knew there had to be more, there had to be a way to break free...but at the time, it seemed like an impossible dream. Maybe dreaming too big was a bad thing. Maybe "they" were right. My thoughts of escape were interrupted by the running shower.

Noelle, give up! It's over!

It was clear I was having a breakdown. Everything was falling apart, yet, I couldn't accept defeat. I was not a failure. I was a fighter, a survivor, and the product of numerous powerful generational influences. But that didn't change the fact that I was behind on all of my expenses and was about to lose my home. Years prior, I decided to explore real estate to help build wealth for my family. Little did I know this journey would be more complex than a game of Monopoly — no colorful money and no "pass go." I was confident that real estate would help me become a millionaire, just as it had for so many others. There were statistics reporting that real estate had created 90% of all millionaires in the United States, and that figure was climbing year after year. I had also watched my fair share of popular HGTV shows and seen how much money can be made from fixes and flips. *How difficult could it really be?*

My exposure to real estate began without much hands-on experience, a sound plan, or a mentor. I was ready, or so I thought. I was in my twenties and working full-time when I started flipping and fixing houses. I was able to flip a few and make what I felt was reasonable money. There was a shift in the market and property values were steadily rising. I took advantage of the opportunity to buy (overpay), repair, and resell for profit. This lasted a few years and my financial future was promising.

In June 2007, my world turned upside down. With my lack of knowledge about real estate patterns and danger indicators, I eventually found myself in the midst of the real estate crisis bubble. The housing market plummeted and I lost my job in the middle of four simultaneous flips. The financing fell through, making the hard money debts unmanageable. Despite depleting my savings, and 401k, and attempting to obtain various loans, I was unable to stay up. After exhausting all financial assistance alternatives, I did something that changed the path of my life forever. I swallowed my pride and made one final attempt to salvage my family's house. I contacted the

PICK A HORSE

only person who could financially save me from drowning in the sea of debt.

My great-aunt, Joyce, was my grandfather's sister, someone I had always held a deep affection for. She was the one who had "made it." The first in our family to immigrate from Jamaica to America. She had established herself and had purchased a multi-family home in Connecticut. Aunt Joyce paved the way for her siblings and their children to follow her example and move to the U. S. Every year, my family and I would make the trip to visit her, the matriarch of our family. As the first of my grandmother's children to be born in America, I felt connected to her legacy. I knew I would be able to count on her. Like me, she was a trailblazer and a go-getter. She understood what it meant to go after her dreams and risk everything. She knew what it meant to pull up her bootstraps and bet on a dream, not knowing what the outcome of the risk would be.

What better person to turn to in a time of need? I was desperate. The plan was to ask her to temporarily lend me the money to help me get back on my feet. Before I called her, I must have rehearsed what I would say over a dozen times. I buried my pride and dialed her number, anxiously waiting for her to pick up. When she answered, I immediately started to plead my case to her over the phone. I bared my soul, recounting my tireless efforts, my depleted savings, and my desperation to save the home where my children and I had resided. I expressed my deep desire to retain ownership of my house and keep my family in a stable environment. I reassured her that I would be responsible in repaying her as soon as I could. I was actively seeking opportunities to help me pay the past due mortgage payments of approximately only $5,200.

After my heartfelt plea, there was dead silence. *Awkward.* The silence was broken by a strong Jamaican accent, *"Yuh mad?"* She went on a rant about how she'd be foolish to give me money for a house that I couldn't afford, and how it would only be a waste of her hard-earned money. Instead of expressing empathy, she expressed her disappointment towards me for reaching out. She questioned why I would waste her time by asking her to invest in a home that was obviously beyond my means, given that I'd already lost my other houses and made many poor decisions with my credit and finances.

She continued the Caribbean tongue-lashing and further expressed that providing me with the money would be a terrible investment. If that wasn't enough, she spewed hard truths about my poor decisions and the changes I needed to make in life. It was obvious that asking and

PICK A HORSE

begging her for money was not the solution, and she was not going to help me. I couldn't believe what I was hearing. I didn't have much of a response—I had to listen and wait for the opportunity to hang up.

When the phone call ended, I felt more defeated than ever. She had refused to loan me the money. I didn't know whether to accept what she said or classify the call as a "toxic conversation." *Was it true? Was I gambling with my life?* I stepped into the shower and was overtaken by sadness, frustration, and anger. I couldn't hold back the tears any longer and cried hysterically. I was infuriated with my situation. *How was I going to pay the mortgage and save my home? How was I going to tell the people that looked up to me the most, the ship had sunk?*

When I stepped out of the shower, my legs gave out, and I collapsed holding my pregnant belly. I continued to cry, feeling helpless and dejected. *Maybe I had failed.* Eventually, I gathered the strength to pull myself up and face the reality of our situation. Unfortunately, we lost our home to foreclosure. With nowhere else to turn, I reached out to my parents and they agreed to allow us to move into their basement. Pregnant with our third child, my husband and I packed up our things and made the move back to Connecticut from Atlanta. I have told this story many times—this was a pivotal shift in my journey to becoming a millionaire. The lowest moment I faced in my life combined with the final "no" by my Aunt Joyce transformed me into the person that became a millionaire almost 10 years later.

Becoming financially free is a life-changing decision, unlike any other. It opens up a world of possibilities and opportunities, allowing you to live life on your own terms. When you are financially free, you can focus on what truly matters to you, whether it's spending quality time with loved ones, traveling the world, or giving back to your community. It's that inner struggle to become free that has sent me on a lifelong journey to bring others along with me. The truth is, unless you work towards this freedom, you'll never achieve it. And before you know it, 20, 30, or 40 years would have passed you by while you sit wondering what happened.

When I started writing this book, I thought of the person who's too afraid to take a risk and bet on themselves. I thought about the person who was not born into wealth and most likely will not inherit it. I thought about the single mother, who wants more but doesn't know where to start, and the family who is sitting at the dining room table stressing over mountains of debt they can't pay. I thought of you, the person burning with a desire to be financially independent, who has tried every side hustle, e-commerce business, MLM, and digital product. You have purchased the courses, watched countless YouTube videos, and set up the LLC...but yet you're still in the same place.

The Power to Choose You

Now that we have established why I wrote this book and who I wrote it for, I want you to focus on the importance of choosing YOU! As you read and become inspired about the possibility of becoming wealthy, I want you to hone in on the one area you are going to work on to achieve your financial freedom. My horse of choice has been real estate. You'll need to decide what yours will be and I will discuss more about this in the subsequent chapters. One of the main reasons people don't achieve financial success is they suffer from FOMO. The fear of missing out. They think that if they don't start the next greatest venture, while in the middle of something else, they will miss out. Wealthy people (and that's who you are) don't have this problem. They understand the focus and attention it takes to take something from mediocre to great. Again, we'll discuss this throughout this book, so this is just what I call "whetting your palate."

YOU HAVE THE POWER TO CHOOSE

Can I ask you a few personal questions? How much is your freedom worth to you? Do you want to be caught in a never-ending, "barely enough" cycle in which many people find themselves? Are you willing to do whatever it takes to break the cycles of financial mediocrity? One of the books that has been pivotal to my success is *Rich Dad, Poor Dad* by Robert Kiyosaki. In the book, Mr. Kiyosaki contrasts the financial philosophies of two father figures in his life. The "Rich Dad" character, a friend's father, exemplifies a mindset focused on creating wealth through entrepreneurship, investing, and financial education.

In contrast, the "Poor Dad," the author's biological father, represents a more traditional approach of working for a paycheck, saving, and avoiding risks. In the book, Kiyosaki shares key lessons on building wealth such as the importance of financial literacy, investing in assets, and developing a mindset of financial independence. The book challenges conventional beliefs about money and offers a fresh perspective on achieving wealth. When you think about those two fathers— which one are you? Are you the poor dad—whose focus was on just doing enough to get by with no financial plan? Or the rich dad—whose focus was creating financial wealth and freedom? *Can I give you a slight nudge and suggest which one you <u>should</u> choose?* Go for the latter.

PICK A HORSE

When I was younger, my grade schoolteacher often encouraged us to put on our "thinking caps" when a new concept or a different way to view things was introduced. This is the time for you to put on your "Wealth Thinking Cap." From this time forward, I don't want you to think about the limitations you are facing today. I don't want you to think about what areas you are lacking in. In fact, I want you to hit delete—just like you would on a computer and remove the old data. Delete everything you have learned up to this point, as that knowledge has not led you to where you need to be. I want you to keep on your thinking cap. Achieving wealth is going to require your total focus and a growth plan. You have to see yourself being wealthy before it happens. You must believe that it can and will happen for you, even if you have failed in the past. I also want you to be willing to walk away from anything that will become a distraction. When I began my real estate entrepreneurial journey, I was juggling a stressful full-time corporate job. Admittedly, it was difficult for me to balance life. I was a wife, mother, corporate vice president, and a real estate investor. I was tired.

As I began to grow my real estate business, I often found myself exhausted after working so many long hours for someone else. This is why I have always been an advocate of full-time entrepreneurship, where you can create your own schedule that fits with your values and lifestyle. Having a corporate job can make you feel like you are stuck in a never-ending cycle of to-do lists, crazy deadlines, and the constant fear of getting the boot. It can make you compromise spending time at your children's basketball game while instead, you settle to attend another important company meeting. Then there's the powerlessness of not knowing what's next and always worrying about being let go or being moved around. Let's be honest—it's stressful.

Entrepreneurship, when done properly, can offer you the opportunity to take control of your destiny and be independent. When you hunt, you eat—and you eat well. While corporate jobs may seem to provide a sense of security for some, they often limit the financial freedom and personal fulfillment that you want to achieve. In other words, there is generally a cap that your position will earn. Ultimately, the choice between entrepreneurship and traditional employment lies in your desire for freedom, self-reliance, and the pursuit of personal and professional growth—without any restrictions.

I have always been an advocate of taking a chance on yourself. Choosing to invest in your own abilities rather than relying on others or external ideas will ultimately be more rewarding and purposeful. Don't be afraid of the

PICK A HORSE

unknown. The unknown is why many people run back when things get hard. However, the unknown is what builds character, resilience, and the quest for knowledge to become better. If you truly believe you deserve more, you won't quit in the face of adversity.

I know what it's like to hit rock bottom with no one to rescue you. It is devastating! That moment on my bathroom floor is the reason I have dedicated myself to helping others achieve wealth the right way. This book is inspired by my journey and life lessons. It's a combination of things I have been coached and mentored in by some of the best experts, and what I have read. It also includes personal experiences of what works and what doesn't. This is also a comprehensive account from a black Caribbean woman's perspective in a male-dominated field that has experienced more prejudices than I care to mention. What I am saying is if I can do it—so can you.

It's time for you to decide to take your wealth journey seriously. Are you going to fearlessly pursue everything you know you deserve, or are you going to continue to allow others to dictate the fate of your and your family's life? There is an urgency in your decision, as there is a widening wealth gap in our society, with the rich becoming richer and the poor becoming poorer. Regardless of

YOU HAVE THE POWER TO CHOOSE

your current income level, being average or mediocre is not going to help you live the life you deserve. Playing small and average may earn you the gold pen at your corporate retirement, but it will not allow you to live your golden life. I know that feeling all too well, and despite being accomplished in Corporate America, I wanted the freedom that could only be achieved by owning my time, deciding how much wealth I would attain, and ultimately deciding my future.

As you read this book, I want you to examine where your life is today. Are you happy with what you have achieved? Do you believe there is more? Are you ready to take charge of your time and finances, as they are the key to achieving true freedom? The wealth gap in America has been a longstanding issue with significant implications for economic inequality and social mobility. "In the third quarter of 2023, 66.6 percent of the total wealth in the United States was owned by the top 10 percent of earners. In comparison, the lowest 50 percent of earners only owned 2.6 percent of the total wealth."[1] This indicates a growing concentration of wealth among the wealthiest individuals. Closing the wealth gap and addressing disparities is crucial.

As wealth is amassed by the wealthiest, it raises questions about income inequality, social mobility, and the

PICK A HORSE

overall health of the economy. For the average person, this could mean limited access to resources and opportunities, making it more challenging to improve one's financial situation and achieve long-term financial security. So, what does this mean for you? Every day that you don't make a decision and move towards securing the bag, you are losing. In today's world, it's super critical for you to become an active participant in the wealth game. This means being smart with money choices, putting your money into things that grow in value, and always looking for ways to level up and move forward.

By taking charge of your financial journey, you set yourself up to handle the money hurdles that come with the rich-poor divide and build a solid and successful future for you and your family. You may be saying, "This all sounds great Noelle, but I feel lost and don't know where to begin." Once you learn how to achieve wealth, you will never be able to turn it off. Trust me. Don't try to figure it all out on your own. At this juncture, let's not worry about the how's. Let's focus on the why's. Ask yourself these questions.

Why do I need to become wealthy?

Why do I need to focus on entrepreneurship?

Why do I need to do this now?

Do I have a good relationship with money?

Throughout your wealth journey, as you continue to grow and learn you will evolve into the person you are meant to be. No matter where you are or what fears you have today, I hope that you push for what you deserve—no matter what. The life you deserve is waiting for you beyond your fears. See your fears as steppingstones toward a brighter future, and watch as you soar to new heights you never thought possible.

Chapter Review

○ Becoming financially free is a life-changing decision, unlike any other. It opens up a world of possibilities and opportunities, allowing you to live life on your own terms.

○ One of the main reasons people don't achieve financial success is they suffer from FOMO. The fear of missing out.

○ Achieving wealth is going to require your total focus and a growth plan. You have to see yourself being wealthy before it happens. You must believe that it can and will happen for you, even if you have failed in the past.

○ Entrepreneurship, when done properly, can offer you the opportunity to take control of your destiny and be independent.

YOU HAVE THE POWER TO CHOOSE

Your Free Gift

SCAN HERE

Noelle's Free Gift

NoellesFreeGift.com

CHAPTER TWO

Survival of the Fittest: From Employee to Business Owner

THE DAY FINALLY arrived for us to move into my parent's basement. It was one of my most humbling moments. I felt like a failure. To add more flame to the fire, being pregnant with my third child triggered even more emotions and created more friction. I was a mess! I had lost all faith in myself. Moving back home presented additional challenges for my entrepreneurial pursuits. My parents and I weren't on the same page about entrepreneurship and me pursuing real estate. At that time, I was a college dropout, and they wanted me to re-enroll to finish the degree I walked away from after my third year.

I was raised in a traditional Jamaican working-class home and education was always stressed as a means to stability in life. My parents held traditional jobs and worked hard to give us a middle-class life. Leaving school and becoming a real estate investor went against my parents' philosophies of what a good life should include for me. To them, my choices appeared reckless. Although they wanted the best for me, they didn't understand I was cut differently. I was living under their roof, so I obliged. Upon returning home, I enrolled at the University of Connecticut to continue my education. But I couldn't shake the feeling that real estate was what I needed to be doing. It was my destiny.

One day while listening to the radio, I heard a commercial advertisement about a free real estate investing class in my area and decided to attend. The class was very informative. It educated me on things I didn't know about real estate investing. Attending the class opened my eyes to all the mistakes I had made while fixing and flipping houses. Although I had experienced some success, I soon discovered that I had so much more to learn. It felt good to enter those rooms and soak up the knowledge from real estate investors that were profitable.

The rooms were somewhat intimidating at first—those investors were closing big contracts, but I didn't let being "the little one in the room" stop me. The classes opened a whole new world of possibilities and taught me how to acquire properties at a discount and make a profit. The investors taught me a more cost-efficient way to make repairs instead of buying materials sold at full price from local hardware stores. Attending those classes was the beginning of me envisioning greater. I believed that life could be more fulfilling, and I didn't have to accept where I was. They helped me find my stride and recover from my previous failure.

I continued to take additional classes, learning more about wholesaling, joint ventures, private placement memos, hard money, and private money lenders, and raising funds for real estate deals. The classes also taught me how I should structure a deal. All of these topics were foreign to me. It was this combination of education, knowledge, new relationships, and being in the room with successful people that opened my eyes to what was possible. I had been doing it all wrong. I was following what I thought was the right thing to do based on what I had seen on television. The rooms stretched me to see the changes I needed to make to transition into profitable entrepreneurship.

There was a complete transformation to my mindset and my thought process. The investors showed me how to be a hunter and become self-sufficient. I was convinced that I was capable of feeding myself and creating my own opportunities without relying on a job or family members to rescue me. Building my confidence, I believed that I possessed the potential to achieve great things. I could do this in this new world, filled with new people, education, and information, which could open for me if I took the first step. One day it was as if a light bulb had switched on. My great-aunt's refusal to lend me money was the best thing that could have happened to me. I had to lose my last house, hit rock bottom, experience foreclosure, and file for bankruptcy to arrive at this place of self-revelation. Although it was a challenging and embarrassing time, it was my "re-birth." This was the moment I became Noelle Randall, the businesswoman, CEO, and millionaire.

Who Do You Need to Become?

Entrepreneurship is often described as a powerful self-development journey that brings out the best *or worst* in individuals. Unlike working for others, where one can feel like a caged animal being told what to do and when to do it, being an entrepreneur provides a sense of liberation

PICK A HORSE

and ownership over one's time and income. This freedom, however, comes with responsibilities and challenges, as personal growth and discipline play crucial roles in the entrepreneurial path. Venturing into entrepreneurship offers a different kind of freedom. It allows individuals to take charge of their lives, time, and income. Unlike in a corporate setting, where income is typically capped, entrepreneurship provides the opportunity to expand financially. Having faced multiple layoffs while working in the banking and mortgage banking industry, I have experienced the lack of control that comes with corporate America, firsthand. The uncertainty of suddenly losing a job due to departmental restructuring or company closures can be unsettling.

Reflecting on my entrepreneurial journey, I am thankful for the opportunities that have been afforded to me as I have taken on the responsibility of educating myself on what it means to become financially free. Minorities and women have undeniably made significant progress in their net worth and will continue to do so in the future. This progress is largely a result of self-investment through educating ourselves on wealth accumulation and entrepreneurship. By increasing our level of ownership of businesses, women, in particular, have been able to advance in society. I am no stranger to hardships. I have faced many financial struggles, being a single parent, and having my own share of life's obstacles, but I don't allow those hardships to define me. We are defined by our dreams and goals, not our struggles.

When embarking on the journey of entrepreneurship, especially as a transitioning employee, challenges are inevitable. A significant reason why many business owners face difficulties transitioning from an employee mindset to an entrepreneurial one is the failure to undergo a fundamental shift in perspective. When you decide to become your own boss, it's important that you shift your mindset from employee to employer. In the book, *E-Myth Mastery: The Seven Essential Disciplines for Building a World-Class Company* by Michael E. Gerber, it talks about how many new business owners end up stuck just working as employees in their business because they try to do everything by themselves. As an employee, you typically function as an individual contributor, completing assigned tasks in exchange for compensation. However, the role of an entrepreneur demands a different outlook. While you may leverage skills acquired as an employee, entrepreneurship requires a shift in mindset towards creation rather than mere implementation.

Success in entrepreneurship extends beyond just working for yourself. It's about creating businesses that can run on their own, so you can keep making money even when you're not there. Being your own boss is a big part of being a successful entrepreneur, unlike being an employee who just focuses on getting paid for their work. It's not just a job—it's a lifestyle; so, it's important to make sure your goals align with what you really want. To create wealth, you must think like the wealthy. Instead of doing tasks they don't enjoy doing that take valuable time from their workday, they delegate. As you think about your new or existing small business, create a list of who you need on your team. This change lets you create a business that doesn't rely only on you, which could mean big things like selling your business down the road.

From Scarcity to Abundance

One day, I confronted the harsh truth within myself that I had a scarcity mindset. It was that mindset that kept me in a job three years longer than I should have stayed. It kept me thinking that I needed to be reliant on direct deposits. Although I appeared to have financial security, it came at the cost of my personal freedom, time, and sanity. I could no longer overlook the limitations tied to this perceived financial stability. Truthfully, I had no control over my time, earnings, and professional path; my job had that control. A scarcity mindset is a belief that there are not enough opportunities or resources to fund your dream life. It is characterized by a fear of lack or limitation, leading to feelings of competition, comparison, and hoarding. This mindset can prevent you from taking risks or pursuing your dreams due to a deep-seated belief that there is not enough to go around, so you must hold onto what you have.

For example, someone with a scarcity mindset may be hesitant to transition from being an employee to a business owner because they fear the uncertainty and risk involved. They may worry that they will not be able to find enough customers, generate sufficient income, or compete with established businesses. This fear of failure and belief that success is limited can hold them back from taking the leap into entrepreneurship, even if they have a great business idea and the skills to succeed.

Think about where you are today. Does a scarcity mindset keep you believing that you can't take the leap? By shifting to an abundance mindset—believing in the potential for growth, opportunities, and success—you can overcome the limitations of scarcity thinking and take the necessary steps towards becoming a successful business owner. Entrepreneurship offers you the freedom you need. It offers the ability to have your own products and services, and make unlimited income. You

PICK A HORSE

can enjoy the fruits of your labor, with the income being paid directly to you.

Starting a business is much easier today than it was when I started. Information for new business owners wasn't as readily available, and the initial start-up was a challenge. Setting up the proper structure, learning about LLCs, and creating a website were just a few of the unknown territories for me. I had no idea about how to attract customers. There was also the challenge of managing my bills because I lacked the confidence to maintain a steady stream of income from my business. All of these factors required a significant investment of time, effort, and resources to learn and master. Thankfully, I did!

You may be wondering if you can become a successful entrepreneur. The answer is, Yes! I believe that anyone can be successful in business. Success in entrepreneurship is not limited to a specific personality type or educational background. Whether you are an introvert or an extrovert, have a sixth-grade education, or hold a PhD, there are common traits that can contribute to your success. One key attribute is resilience—the ability to bounce back from setbacks and keep pushing forward. The entrepreneurial journey is not a smooth one; it requires dedication, commitment, and a willingness to persevere in the face of challenges.

Your Belief in YOU!

The lesson that my great-aunt taught me was incredibly powerful, and it still resonates with me today. It is a big reason why I have been able to achieve success. That discussion with her changed my life. After attending the classes and learning more about what is required to be wealthy, I realized that she was right. I was blindly investing in real estate based on the limited knowledge I had. There was so much to learn as a real estate investor and business owner. If she would have lent me the money, it would have been a band-aid instead of fixing the real problem.

By refusing to lend me money to save my home, she was saving me from myself. The truth is I wasn't ready and it wouldn't have been a wise investment. At the time, I was stuck in a poverty mindset and operating at a low frequency, which prevented me from seeing the bigger picture. Later, as I surrounded myself with new people and learned more, I became more confident in myself and my abilities. I became more knowledgeable and learned the business of real estate.

PICK A HORSE

When I spoke to her again, I apologized for asking her to loan me the money and acknowledged the truth of her words. She was so impressed with my growth that she became my first investor by offering some money to invest in my real estate coaching. That investment paid off when I was able to use my newfound knowledge to make successful real estate deals and eventually pay her back. I am so happy she saw the potential and I took her up on her offer. I knew I needed a real estate coach.

Despite being broke, bankrupt, living in my parents' basement, and struggling to make ends meet, I needed to invest in more coaching. The investment was $20,000, with a $3,000 initial payment and monthly installments thereafter. To make that initial payment, I took a risk and cancelled one of my classes at the University of Connecticut and applied my refund to the coaching. Though I do not recommend this approach to others, it worked for me. Real Estate coaching proved to be one of the most transformative things I have ever done for myself. My coach taught me not only about wholesaling but also about mindset and the importance of finding people's problems to solve.

Reflecting on this time of my life reminds me of the evolution that we all must make to become the best version of ourselves. I was recently asked what it required at every

SURVIVAL OF THE FITTEST: FROM EMPLOYEE TO BUSINESS OWNER

stage of my life to transition from a six to multiple seven-figure earner. I shared that each level, in both my career and later my business, required a different version of myself. I had to release limiting beliefs, become more educated, learn how to communicate, and acquire the skills necessary to attract more wealth. While working in corporate America, I transitioned from simply holding a job to climbing the corporate ladder, progressing from earning $40,000 to $50,000, $60,000, and $75,000 per year. I eventually broke into the realm of six figures, earning $150,000 to $200,000 annually. My last corporate title was vice president with earnings of $225,000 yearly. Many key advancements marked a shift from being an employee making five figures to a manager earning six figures.

While earning six figures, it was imperative to embody the characteristics of an individual adept at mastering business concepts, excelling as a manager, and embracing leadership responsibilities. I had to demonstrate my capability of achieving the company's expected projections. This transition demanded a commitment to studying leadership and management principles earnestly. I progressed from being an employee to a manager and eventually to a leader who could effectively delegate tasks. There were crucial lessons I learned on this journey, which enabled me to achieve financial success in the six, seven, and beyond seven-figure range that we will discuss throughout this book.

To reach higher levels, it is essential to master a few areas including the art of influence, the art of communication, and the art of leadership. Through these practices, I advanced from a manager to vice president at prestigious financial institutions like Bank of America and Chase Bank. Earning high-paying six-figure positions required me to excel in the skill of supervising others and transforming from just a manager to a genuine leader. Throughout the progression, there were levels of elevation from being an individual contributor to a manager, and eventually securing the level of vice president, responsible for both direct and indirect reports.

The Art of Influence: Involves using your influence to manage and monitor progress, setting clear expectations for success, and providing support to ensure tasks are completed satisfactorily. When you understand and master this area, you realize you don't need to resort to force to get people to follow you.

The Art of Communication: Mastering the art of communication within various levels of an organization is important for your professional and business growth. There are different communication styles for upper management, direct reports, as well as senior management, and C-suite. Learning to tailor my message upwards and downwards was pivotal in my journey. Developing effective communication skills became crucial, especially in delivering messages to employees with transparency while still maintaining confidentiality about company matters. As I progressed through levels of leadership, I learned how to adapt my communication style depending on who I was talking to.

From the corporate world to the business world, the art of communication is paramount. Effective communication is the foundation of every aspect of business, from pitching ideas to clients, leading team meetings, negotiating deals, to providing feedback to colleagues. It is the key to building strong relationships, fostering collaboration, and ensuring clarity in all interactions. Clear and concise communication helps in avoiding misunderstandings and conflicts, leading to increased productivity and efficiency within an organization. Being able to convey your message in a way that is easily understood by others is needed to achieve goals and objectives. Furthermore, strong communication skills can enhance your credibility, influence, and overall professional image, making it easier to network, build partnerships, and advance in business.

The Art of Leadership: Transitioning from a six-figure income earner to a seven-figure one marked a significant shift in my financial trajectory. It wasn't until I ventured into entrepreneurship that I achieved this milestone, as the corporate realm did not afford me the same financial opportunities. From my own journey in the corporate world, I've learned that infusing elements of what I learned throughout my professional career into my business endeavors truly enhanced my business growth.

As a new business owner, you may feel unprepared with the necessary skills for success, which can contribute to your reservations about taking the leap into entrepreneurship. However, I hold a different perspective. Through your experiences in various workplace environments, you have had the opportunity to witness both effective and ineffective practices. You have observed workflows, standard operating procedures, competent managers, and those who fall short. By reflecting on these observations, you can identify the areas where you excel. While you may not have expertise in every aspect of business, it is important to recognize the depth of your knowledge and insights gained from your experiences.

Reflection: Think about the skills and training you have received in your current or previous workplaces.

How can you integrate your experiences from your professional career to optimize different areas of your company?

How can you apply your knowledge of successful company management to streamline operations and enhance efficiency within your business?

How can you utilize your understanding of workplace culture to cultivate a strong organizational culture that aligns with your business values and goals?

As I transitioned, I began by doing what I knew how to do well, and then I hired coaches, read books, and attended courses to help me learn in the areas where there was a deficit. In your first few years, you will not know every aspect of running a business. My leadership training in corporate America was helpful for some of the day-to-day operations, however, it was my responsibility to take it further by attaining more comprehensive knowledge of all my organization's components. Yes, it's true that transitioning to entrepreneurship is not always easy. While you possess management acumen and the ability to make personnel decisions, delving into creating your own company reveals a multitude of unfamiliar territories such as website functionality, backend operations, merchant processing, credit card disputes, and various other facets that come with being an owner. Additionally, assuming the role of the business's public face and brand adds a new layer of complexity to the challenge.

Despite the learning curve, I am proof that it can be done. It may take some time to build the belief in yourself to step out into full-time entrepreneurship, so be patient with your process. For some, the process may be gradual. Focusing on your personal development alongside building your business skills is critical to shift your mindset. It took me three years to finally quit my job, and looking back, I realize that if I had been more consistent with certain actions, I could have expedited the process. Today, I have been a full-time entrepreneur for over six years and have owned FDR Horizons for a decade now, since its establishment on January 10th, 2014.

Lose the Employee Mentality

One major mindset shift that can hinder success for new entrepreneurs is maintaining an employee mentality. Operating with the mindset of a zoo animal waiting to be fed, rather than a hunter who seeks out opportunities, will hold you back. As an entrepreneur, you need to be proactive, resilient to rejection, and willing to continuously pursue your goals. Just like a lion in the wild facing unsuccessful hunts most of the time, in business, you would likely face rejection in your endeavors. It's crucial to not take these rejections personally, but instead view them as stepping stones towards achieving your ultimate objectives. Embracing an optimistic mindset and understanding that each rejection brings you closer to success, can help you navigate the challenges of entrepreneurship with confidence and resilience.

It's Not Personal!

A major lesson I learned in my pivot into business ownership was to not take anything personally. In *The Four Agreements* by Don Miguel Ruiz, the second agreement is, "Don't Take Anything Personally." In the world of business, you will encounter numerous challenges, criticisms, and rejections. It's important to understand that these are often not a reflection of your worth or abilities, but rather part of the natural ups and downs of entrepreneurship. By not taking things personally, you can maintain a clear focus on your goals, learn from feedback, and keep moving forward with resilience and determination. Remember, business success often involves facing setbacks with a positive mindset and using them as opportunities for growth and improvement. Achieving success as an entrepreneur involves understanding that not everyone you reach out to will become a customer. It's common to have a large number of subscribers but only a fraction of them will convert into clients. You must accept this reality and shift away from an employee mindset where every action has a predictable outcome. Embracing the uncertainties of entrepreneurship and developing a comfort with the idea that setbacks are part of the journey is essential for long-term success.

Become a Student - Personal Growth and Development

To develop the skills needed to thrive as an entrepreneur, it's essential to make your personal development a priority. Invest in classes, seminars, and conferences that focus on entrepreneurship to enhance your knowledge and skills. Surround yourself with a network of success-

SURVIVAL OF THE FITTEST: FROM EMPLOYEE TO BUSINESS OWNER

ful entrepreneurs to learn from their experiences and insights. As a business professional, you should always be seeking to enhance your skills. Venture beyond your comfort zone and actively participate in industry classes, workshops, and events that challenge you to grow. While online learning and webinars offer convenience, there is unparalleled value in attending these gatherings in person, attending events where you can network and learn hands-on. Whether you're in real estate, the hair industry, landscaping, food, social media, photography, videography, or any other field, immersing yourself in the right environment can help you refine your skills and grow your business.

Balancing the entrepreneurial aspects of running a business with personal growth is important for long-term success, and dedicating time each day to both areas, even if just in small increments, can accelerate your journey toward achieving your goals. Transitioning from earning a six-figure income to reaching seven-figures included cultivating my self-motivation, exerting the same level of effort for my own business as I did when working for others, and adhering to high standards without external supervision.

Achieving seven figures necessitates a mindset focused on self-discipline, determination, and the ability to per-

PICK A HORSE

severe through tough times. Setting clear financial goals and actively working towards them is crucial in making the leap from a six-figure income to a seven-figure success. When it comes to managing your own business, the level of effort required increases significantly. This shift in dedication and perseverance is what propels one from earning six figures to reaching seven figures.

Entrepreneurship demands much more than just proficiency in accounting, marketing, or sales. It's about the resiliency to press on through the inevitable challenges that arise. It's about being authentic and finding your passion in your business. It's about being honest with yourself and where your weaknesses lie. It's about bossing up and taking responsibility when things don't work out as planned. It's also about having a vision and learning how to lead others.

Questions to reflect on:

On your journey to building your business, what characteristics do you need to increase?

SURVIVAL OF THE FITTEST: FROM EMPLOYEE TO BUSINESS OWNER

Do you struggle with an employee mentality?

Do you have a problem delegating tasks? Do you feel that you must do everything yourself?

On a scale of 1-10, how would you rate your communication level?

Have you discovered the best communication levels for different organizational tiers?

Chapter Review

○ Entrepreneurship demands much more than just proficiency in accounting, marketing, or sales. It's about the resiliency to persevere through the inevitable challenges that arise.

○ A significant reason why many business owners face difficulties transitioning from an employee mindset to an entrepreneurial one is the failure to undergo a fundamental shift in perspective.

○ A scarcity mindset is a belief that there are not enough opportunities or resources to fund your dream life. It is characterized by a fear of lack or limitation, leading to feelings of competition, comparison, and hoarding.

○ To reach higher levels of success, it is essential to master a few areas—the art of influence, the art of communication, and the art of leadership.

○ Effective communication is the foundation of every aspect of business, from pitching ideas to clients, leading team meetings, negotiating deals, to providing feedback to colleagues. It is the key to building strong relationships, fostering collaboration, and ensuring clarity in all interactions.

CHAPTER THREE
You Can't Hide

"To say that I am ashamed is an extreme understatement," said Uber CEO, Billionaire Travis Kalanick. "My job as your leader is to lead ... and that starts with behaving in a way that makes us all proud. That is not what I did, and it cannot be explained away."[2] Previous to this statement, Kalanick engaged in a heated argument over wages with an Uber driver that went viral. Once the video surfaced, Mr. Kalanick had no choice but to make an apology to the public.

"It's clear this video is a reflection of me – and the criticism we've received is a stark reminder that I must fundamentally change as a leader and grow up," he added. "This is the first time I've been willing to admit that I need leadership help and I intend to get it."[2]

PICK A HORSE

One of the notions I stand by strongly is that who you are as a person (your character) will eventually surface in your business. Many business leaders try to build the business without building themselves as well. It may seem to work out for a while, but without fail, who they truly are will rise to the surface and be exhibited in their behavior. Had Kalanick spent more time working on his emotional intelligence behind the scenes, I believe he would have been able to keep his cool when he was confronted by the driver.

So, what does it really require of you to grow a successful profitable business? That's a great question! It not only requires a shift in educating yourself but it also entails an upleveling in your behavior. I am re-reading a book that I read some time ago that discusses this very topic titled, *What Got You Here, Won't Get You There* by Marshall Goldsmith. The book discusses the behavioral transitions that leaders must make to become great. If you want to achieve record-breaking milestones and increase your net worth, Goldsmith challenges you to check your behaviors.

He also emphasizes that while intelligence, skillset, and knowledge may have propelled you to your current level of success, surpassing seven figures requires a deeper understanding and refinement of your behaviors. This transition signifies a pivotal shift from relying solely on your technical expertise to honing interpersonal skills and leadership qualities.

It's undeniable that during Mr. Kalanick's tenure at Uber, the company had significant success. Uber grew under Kalanick's leadership and launched services, such as UberEATS and UberPOOL, and expanded into new markets around the world. Despite his success, investors forced Mr. Kalanick to resign as chief executive in 2017, after a series of privacy scandals and complaints of discrimination and sexual harassment at the company.[3]

Progressing from one level to the next often hinges on one's behaviors. A key area of growth, that has enabled me to achieve even greater success, is managing my emotions. As an entrepreneur with numerous responsibilities, including being a parent and experiencing the changes that come with aging and hormonal shifts, mastering my emotions has been crucial, and I can admit I haven't always been the best at this. Balancing the roles of entrepreneur, multimillionaire, real estate investor, author, speaker, and more, while navigating the unique emotional challenges that come with being a woman, has taught me the importance of emotional intelligence.

PICK A HORSE

In the past, I made the mistake of selecting team members and leaders based on their ability to handle my emotions, which as time progressed, proved to be a hindrance. At times, I would become emotionally overwhelmed during meetings due to the disarray in our business operations. For instance, during one meeting, my team disclosed that our accounts receivables were in a state of chaos. While we should have collected $200,000 that month, only $90,000 had been collected, and $80,000 was past due with no follow-up action plans in place. Despite our company being owed these amounts based on contracts, there had been no efforts to pursue the payments. On the contrary, our company bills were promptly paid on the accounts payable side, while our outstanding invoices remained unpaid. Angrily, I gathered my team members in a meeting and expressed my frustrations by raising my voice and using harsh language, behaving in a manner unbecoming of a good manager.

As a CEO, reflecting on my past behavior, I realize that there were more constructive ways to handle situations that arose. Rather than expressing frustration towards messengers delivering unwelcome news, I should have approached these instances with greater composure and understanding. It became clear that in order to sustain a seven-figure business successfully, I needed to address and modify these behaviors.

My business suffered a significant blow due to my actions. In a particular year, we generated around 3.6 million in revenue, but the following year we saw a drop to 1.6 million. This decline was a direct result of my inaccessibility. I had entrusted someone with inadequate leadership, management, and accounting skills, and was clearly unqualified to oversee a multi-million-dollar enterprise. Despite these shortcomings, this individual excelled in handling my emotional needs, allowing me to express myself freely, be comforted, apologize, and move forward.

While I appreciated this dynamic at the time, it resulted in the ultimate detriment to my business's performance. Attaining financial success is one thing; maintaining it consistently and repeatedly is a different challenge altogether. If I wanted to turn my business around from the quick dive down, I needed to acknowledge my actions, make necessary changes, and commit to continuous growth and improvement. I needed to take responsibility and steer the ship back to safety. Despite making mistakes along the way, I have learned valuable lessons that have contributed to my personal and professional development. Today, when confronted with negativity, I strive not to direct it back at the person delivering it. Being approachable and available in my business is a priority for me. Whether it's writing books or creating content, these tasks are integral to my business, particularly in maintaining the image and essence of the Noelle Randall brand. However, there are moments when external challenges can affect my emotional state, hindering my ability to produce content effectively. During these times, I may need to limit my accessibility to ensure the quality of my work remains consistent with my brands.

As I revisited the book *What Got You Here Won't Get You There*, I was once again reminded of the negative behaviors that can hinder our progress to the next level. It's often our behaviors that act as barriers to our growth rather than a lack of skills or intellectual knowledge since these are what initially propelled us to our current position. While our existing knowledge and abilities have brought us this far, it is our behavior that will ultimately propel us to the next level. The experiences you gain along the way will help shape you into a more resilient and stronger individual. Every successful sale you make will boost your confidence, while every setback will require you to dig deep and confront deficiencies or feelings of lack of self-worth. However, with each hurdle you overcome, you will become stronger and more confident in your abilities. The key to becoming a successful entrepreneur is to stay the course and continue learning from your experiences so that you can emerge better and stronger.

Overcome Your Fears

In 2009, when I re-entered the real estate market, I had to overcome the failures of the 2007 financial crisis. Subconsciously, I knew that if I let the fear of failure hold me back, I would miss out on the millions of dollars that awaited me in the future. However, I needed to connect that to my actions. I had to work on myself and overcome those inner issues that had been built around the words spoken by those whom I loved and trusted. I had to ask myself hard questions. *Did I believe what they had said,* or *did I believe I was capable of truly becoming successful?* I learned to block out my fears, focus on my goals, and look forward to the promising future. After jumping into the entrepreneurship pool again, I eventually gained the confidence to run a full-time business. I learned how to make a profit in my real estate business from my parent's basement while working with my real estate coach. The skills I learned eventually allowed me to move out and rebuild my life. Once I graduated from the University of Connecticut, I relocated to Atlanta where I continued to pursue real estate. I didn't immediately leave my full-time job. I still had to overcome the devastation of the previous loss. The fear of failing again cemented a level of fear in me that limited my ability to fully embrace taking the leap.

In times of distress, it's easy to feel weighed down, almost like gravity is pulling you under. By implementing mental, emotional, and spiritual practices, you can find the strength to lift yourself up. Regardless of religious beliefs, having a strong sense of connection to something greater than yourself can be empowering. Understanding that there are unseen forces at work and believing in the potential for miracles to occur can shift your perspective. By maintaining a positive mindset and recognizing the influence of your thoughts on your reality, you can align yourself with the law of attraction. This principle emphasizes that similar energies attract each other, and the intentions you set can manifest into tangible outcomes. Embracing these concepts, regardless of your faith, can propel you toward personal and professional growth.

Self-perception

My second mentor, whom I met in 2017, helped me learn how to trust myself and to be firm in my decision-making. She introduced me to using self-affirmations, to remind myself every day that I was a smart, brilliant, worthy person, who made good life and business decisions. This positive self-talk helped me to change how I saw myself and allowed me to make decisions more confidently.

As you embark on your wealth journey, reflect on how you really see yourself.

Do you trust your decision-making abilities?

Do you struggle with your self-worth?

Do you suffer with survivor's guilt?

Survivor's guilt is a complex emotional experience that can arise when an individual achieves financial success while others around them continue to struggle or face hardship. This often stems from a sense of unworthiness or discomfort at benefiting disproportionately compared to others. I remember one time when I overworked myself to take care of others. I don't mean my husband and kids; I am referring to the people who often made me feel as if it was my responsibility to pay their phone or light bill. And those who often asked me for a handout because "I had it." It was not a good feeling to be the person that people called solely because they needed something, and

PICK A HORSE

not because they truly cared about my well-being. Over time I had to learn how to set up boundaries. I had to learn that I wasn't going to be indebted to anyone simply because they wouldn't dig themselves out of the financial dungeon they had placed themselves in.

As you become successful, you will most likely experience those who feel entitled to your wealth. You'll have to turn on your B.S. meter to detect those who you should and shouldn't rescue. Whatever you decide, let it be your true desire and not one that you have been guilted into. Financial manipulation and abuse are real. You must learn to protect yourself. My journey with money taught me that external validation and material possessions are not the answer to inner fulfillment. While I initially believed that showering my loved ones with gifts would prove my worth and earn their approval, I eventually realized that true happiness comes from self-acceptance and personal growth. Buying expensive gifts for my family or trying to showcase my success only served to highlight my insecurities and need for validation.

It was a humbling experience to recognize that lasting happiness cannot be purchased and that my relationships should be built on genuine connections rather than material exchanges. This revelation taught me a valuable life lesson, and that is, money isn't the key to happiness. While it can certainly make life easier and provide opportunities to help others, if you haven't done the inner work to understand your motivations for wanting wealth, it can lead to unforeseen challenges. Money can come and it can vanish quickly, the response to both occurrences, often amplifies the personal issues we carry within us. For instance, if you have a tendency towards addictive behaviors, suddenly having a lot of money can exacerbate those tendencies. Similarly, if you are a people pleaser, you may find yourself giving away money in an attempt to buy affection or approval. In all transparency, I had to acknowledge my reasons for wanting to be wealthy. I had to admit that my desire for wealth was rooted in seeking validation from others. On your journey to wealth, you'll need to assess why you want to be wealthy. Is it to prove *them* wrong? Is it to have other people look and admire you? Or do you want to create financial freedom for yourself and your family?

The Ugly Side of Entrepreneurship

We can't always discuss the highs of entrepreneurship without discussing how to deal with the lows. Many entrepreneurs deal with depression and loneliness. It's common for entrepreneurs to face challenges with their mental health at some point in their business journey. If you struggle in any of these areas, you will need to do the inner work and trust yourself. One simple step to combat this is by practicing positive self-talk and affirmations. Additionally, managing your emotions is key. During my first years in business, I would often feel overwhelmed to the point of breaking down in tears. There were so many things I was experiencing, and I didn't have a healthy outlet to express it. Many of my friends at the time were not experiencing growth in their income and life the way I was, and they couldn't relate to what I was experiencing. While speaking with my mentor one day, she taught me the importance of meditation, expressing how it helps you to control your mind and thoughts. This has helped me avoid spiraling into sadness or depression when things don't go according to plan. Seeking guidance on managing my emotions was one of the best decisions I made.

Mental and Physical Health

Recently I came across an article on LinkedIn that mentioned, "Studies reveal an alarming truth - nearly 72% of entrepreneurs are wrestling with mental health issues. Research from the National Institute of Mental Health reveals that entrepreneurs are 50% more likely to report having a mental health condition."[4]

When you look at these statistics, you can understand the importance of taking care of your mental health. It's not only important to build your mental health but to also take care of your physical health as well. Seventy-six percent of the rich aerobically exercise 30 minutes or more every day," Corley reports in his book, *Change Your Habits, Change Your Life*. "Cardio is not only good for the body, but it's good for the brain," he writes. "Daily aerobic exercise feeds the brain, cleans the brain, and increases your intelligence, each and every time you engage in it."[5]

"Wealthy people value their health," says Corley. In addition to exercising, they watch what they eat, sleep seven or more hours every night, and avoid drinking too much alcohol and watching too much TV."[5]

On this journey, the more that you choose *you*, the more others will try and distract you from that. You must stay grounded and connected to the things that matter most. Those are usually things that money can't buy. For me, that's my husband and kids. This may seem like a simple concept, however, it's so simple that many people miss it.

Think about how many celebrities we have witnessed rise and fall trying to take care of everyone else, and

PICK A HORSE

when they had to file bankruptcy or the money was low, so were their friends.

You will need to consider how you will handle wealth before it is attracted to you. Additionally, it's important to work on insecurities, jealousy, and other negative emotions before the money ever shows up. Entrepreneurs can earn millions and then lose it all because they didn't do the inner work, especially if they never overcame their insecurities, jealousies, or their low-frequency emotions. You have to work on those areas in your life before the money ever shows up, because when it does show up, it won't last. Maintaining mental, emotional, and spiritual stability is paramount for entrepreneurs due to the challenges they face. Building resilience and fortitude is crucial as the business landscape is tough, with a high percentage of ventures failing within the initial years. Focusing on mental strength is key to navigating the inevitable hurdles that arise in the entrepreneurial journey. Each day presents its own set of obstacles, requiring a positive and resilient mindset to persevere through tough times.

Cultivating mental toughness and positivity are not just strategies for success but also lifelines that can help entrepreneurs overcome setbacks and push through difficult moments, ultimately leading them to triumph. The pressures of running a business, and dealing with numerous responsibilities and expectations can be overwhelming. However, you can develop grounding practices to help you cope with those difficult moments. While there is no definitive endpoint to this journey, I remind myself of positive affirmations such as "Everything is always working out for you" and "You are abundant, prosperous, and amazing." It's essential to use affirmations in the first person, such as "I am prosperous" and "I am wealthy," to reinforce self-belief and positivity.

In the fast-paced world of running a business, it can be all too common to neglect the significance of mental and physical health. Just as we dedicate time and effort to maintaining our physical health, it is equally important to nurture our mental well-being. Establishing a daily health regimen can have a profound impact on your overall wellness and productivity as a business owner. By incorporating activities such as mindfulness exercises, meditation, regular breaks, exercise, and seeking professional support when needed, you can enhance your resilience and decision-making abilities, leading to a more fulfilling and successful entrepreneurial journey. Remember, taking care of your health is not just a luxury but a necessity for long-term sustainable success in the business world. A healthy mind is the foundation upon which all your successes are built.

Here is a simple list of things you can do, starting today. Don't ever become too busy to take care of yourself.

- Start your day with mindfulness or meditation to set a positive tone for the day ahead. Even just a few minutes of deep breathing can help calm your mind and reduce stress.

- Make time for activities that bring you joy and relaxation, whether it's reading a book, going for a walk in nature, or practicing a hobby you love.

- Stay connected with loved ones and friends. Social support is crucial for mental well-being. So, make time for meaningful interactions and conversations.

- Prioritize self-care by getting enough sleep, eating nutritious meals, and engaging in regular physical activity. A healthy body contributes to a healthy mind.

- Practice gratitude by keeping a journal and writing down things you are thankful for each day. Focusing on the positive aspects of your life can boost your mood and overall outlook.

- Set boundaries and learn to say no when needed. It's important to prioritize your own needs and well-being, even if it means declining certain commitments.

- Seek professional help if you are struggling with your mental health. Therapy or counseling can provide valuable support and guidance in managing any challenges you may be facing.

Chapter Review

- Progressing from one level to the next often hinges on one's behaviors. A key area of growth that has enabled me to achieve even greater success, is managing my emotions.

- It's often our behaviors that act as barriers to our growth rather than a lack of skills or intellectual knowledge since these are what initially propelled us to our current position.

- The key to becoming a successful entrepreneur is to stay the course and continue learning from your experiences so that you can emerge better and stronger.

- By implementing mental, emotional, and spiritual practices, you can find the strength to lift yourself up.

- Survivor's guilt is a complex emotional experience that can arise when an individual achieves financial success while others around them continue to struggle or face hardship.

- If you haven't done the inner work to understand your motivations for wanting wealth, it can lead to unforeseen challenges.

CHAPTER FOUR
Pick Your Horse and Rein It In

YOU NEVER KNOW who you will meet that will change the course of your life. I first met Lisa Sasevich, "The Queen of Sales Conversations," at an event she was hosting in Fort Lauderdale, Florida. It was the first time I had experienced an event of that magnitude with a confident offer from the host. She presented from the stage to a sold-out room of 200-300 people, sharing her experiences in corporate, being overlooked for promotions, and being capped at a salary. Her words spoke to the core of me. Although she had achieved so much, there was still a level of humility, vulnerability, and compassion that I connected to. Maybe it's because she was a woman with kids, or maybe because there was already this tug-of-war

PICK A HORSE

inside of me as I was searching for more. Either way, I was inspired and in awe of what she had achieved.

Lisa operated a successful business, was a paid speaker, and an author, and ran her own coaching program. She had just celebrated her 50th birthday and showed the audience photos from the glamourous affair—adding to her credibility. Her receipts were undeniable. She was bringing in over $2 million annually. What I earned in a year, she made in just one month. I was truly amazed by her business savvy. That day I watched her close over 100 people, who signed up for her $18,000- $85,000 laser coaching programs. I also signed up—I was convinced I needed her help.

Working with her was the best decision. One of the first pieces of advice she shared with me was, "Pick a Horse and Ride it." She told me that if I didn't stick to one specific path, it would be difficult to reach the millions I wanted to earn. She was right! At the time, I had a hair business, a tea business, and anything else I could put my hand to. I was constantly splitting my time, never fully giving my total attention to any one thing. I had ventured into various business opportunities, making some money here and there, but never reaching the level of a million dollars. She urged me to heed a simple yet powerful principle—to select a single area of focus and dedicate my efforts to it.

I decided that real estate would be the horse that would help me generate wealth. My mentor taught me to fully embrace real estate and get rid of all of the other side businesses that I had, like the hair business, put my children's books aside, get rid of the detox tea that I was selling, and the tiny partnerships I was doing with folks in MLMs and other smaller businesses. So, I started teaching real estate and helping other people to become real-estate millionaires as well. That's where a lot of value was.

By leveraging my expertise in house flipping, I concentrated on this niche, along with managing my rental properties and my income began increasing. By following her advice and concentrating on one core area, I was able to establish a solid foundation in real estate and later expand into additional income streams including teaching and coaching. The key lesson I learned was to commit to a strategy and see it through, akin to picking a horse and riding it to the finish line.

In the fast-paced world of entrepreneurship, the idea of following one course until successful may seem counterintuitive to some. However, history has shown us time and time again that focusing on a singular goal and seeing it through to fruition is a key ingredient to achieving business success. By honing in on *one* course of action, and concentrating your efforts, resources, and energy on mastering your craft and solving challenges, you will ultimately reap the rewards of your hard work.

One notable example of the power of persistence is the story of Thomas Edison and the invention of the light bulb. Despite facing numerous setbacks and failures, Edison remained unwavering in his commitment to his goal. Through tireless experimentation and relentless determination, he eventually succeeded in creating a commercially viable electric light bulb. Ultimately, it is this laser-like focus that sets successful businesses apart and propels them towards long-term growth and prosperity.

Although I am an advocate of real estate, I want you to choose your horse—the one that you are passionate about. I chose real estate because I love it. I discovered it to be simply the most effective way to build wealth. Eighty-nine percent of all millionaires have been made with real estate. It provides numerous practical benefits, such as tax deductions, depreciation, and the ability to write off all of the various expenses. It also hedges against inflation as property values increase. It's a terrific inflation hedge. Again, I love it, and I encourage others to ride it, even if they are doing something else.

I have come across a lot of other incredible entrepreneurs who specialize in hair, landscaping, construction, contractors, flooring, cleaning, law, medicine, and just about every other type of business you can think of, who are not yet making millions of dollars. On the contrary, I've known people who sell rocks, either as appreciation rocks or by painting them, but they make a million dollars.

Essentially, the idea of choosing your horse is to choose something you enjoy that simultaneously makes a lot of money; something you will stick to. It's a horse you enjoy riding. And, while that horse may not initially deliver the wealth you seek or everything you desire, it will if you stay on it, create a plan of action, commit to it, and fall in love with the trip rather than the destination—you can discover your success. I want to add a disclaimer. As the world is changing, especially with the emergence of AI, consider choosing a horse that won't be replaced.

Handle it Like a CEO (Emerging as a Leader)

During my time at Chase Bank, I was able to observe great leadership in the CEO, Jamie Dimon. Mr. Dimon is one of the most successful banking CEOs, with the longest tenure. As of the time of this writing, Chase is one of the most profitable and highly regarded banks, surpassing even Wells Fargo and Bank of America in profitability. Having had the privilege of working as a former employee and vice president at Chase, I can attest to Dimon's exemplary leadership skills. His confident demeanor and articulate speech contribute to him being an exceptional CEO. Whenever he entered a room, he exuded an air of confidence and clarity. He effectively communicated the mission, the various investment opportunities available, and the objectives of different divisions like auto, credit card, and mortgage.

Dimon's strategic vision and focus on customer segmentation, in my opinion, has been viable to the company's success and sets it apart from the competition. He knows exactly which borrowers to target and which ones to avoid. He has a clear understanding of the types of loans that are beneficial for the organization. During my time there, the company did not participate in subprime lending and wasn't heavily involved in government loans, apart from FHA and VA loans. Their core mortgages were based on conventional loans that they could sell off to Freddie Mac and Fannie Mae. The CEO made this decision, clearly communicated it, and always acted accordingly. He had no interest in what other banks were doing and this mindset was shared by middle management and leadership. Our focus was on our own actions and decisions. It's that type of leadership that drives Chase into the #1 ranking for the biggest bank in the United States.[6]

As you transition into your CEO role, it's helpful to model a leader that you admire. Think about what makes them great. What are their qualities? What do you admire about their leadership? What type of culture have they built? What sets their organization apart? Think about these questions and write down the qualities that stand out most to you. How can you add these characteristics to your leadership style and character to help you become a great leader? One of the qualities of successful CEOs like Jeff Bezos of Amazon, Elon Musk of Tesla and X, and Jamie Dimon is their confidence in their company and product. They stand by their product and influence others to do the same. Because of their confidence, when a new product or service is introduced to the market, there is no shortage of buyers. Their vision and focus

PICK A HORSE

create high-in-demand brands. They see the big picture before it becomes big.

When you observe these leaders, you will probably notice they are strong visionaries. If you are having a problem picking your horse, chances are you struggle with a lack of vision. Can I share my thoughts on this? When you are a visionary, you learn how to become laser-focused on what you want to accomplish. Being focused helps you better choose what actions will result in the outcome you want to achieve. Visionaries understand if they have too many things going on at once, it's like trying to ride multiple horses at one time—it can't be done.

> **People who fail to accumulate money, without exception, have the habit of reaching decisions, if at all, very slowly, and of changing these decisions quickly and often."**
>
> — Napoleon Hill

Stand By Your Decision

When I started my entrepreneurial journey, I wasn't good at making a decision. I relied on other people's input all the time. This was a product of my not wanting to take responsibility if things didn't go as planned. That's not my story anymore. Today, I am known for my decisiveness. I am very clear about whether I am in or out.

"Good CEOs realize that a wrong decision may be better than no decision at all." In an article by the *Harvard Business Review*, titled "What Sets Successful CEOs Apart," there was a study conducted, listing the top traits of successful CEOs. Listed at number one was: Deciding with Speed and Conviction. "We discovered that high-performing CEOs do not necessarily stand out for making great decisions all the time; rather, they stand out for being more decisive. They make decisions earlier, faster, and with greater conviction. They do so consistently—even amid ambiguity, with incomplete information, and in unfamiliar domains. People who were described as "decisive" were 12 times more likely to be high-performing CEOs." [7]

In our world, there are a multitude of choices that present themselves to us, bringing blessings and chal-

PICK A HORSE

lenges. Making a decision and standing firm on it is one of the key factors that separate successful people from those who aren't. Successful CEOs are decisive. They don't waver in their choices. They are known for making important decisions that can either make or break a company. They also hold a significant amount of responsibility and are accountable for the outcomes of their decisions. The success of a company depends on the CEO's ability to do this and lead the company in the right direction. Henry Ford is a great example of a visionary who made a decision and stuck by it. He had a vision for Ford Motor Company, and he pushed his engineers to create the machine he wanted. He did not have the technical skills to create it himself, but he knew what he wanted and was determined to make it happen. This is the kind of forward-thinking that makes a successful CEO.

Great CEOs are also good at managing the company's resources. They know when to invest and when to cut back. They understand the market and the competition and can make strategic decisions that keep the company ahead. Being a CEO is a highly demanding job that requires a unique skill set. They are compensated substantially because they carry the responsibility of the organization and are accountable for its outcome. Making sound decisions, managing resources, and having a clear vision for the company are all important traits.

Stay in Alignment

Having a clear vision allows you to say "yes" to the opportunities that are in alignment with what you are building and say "no" to the things that aren't. I am constantly approached with offers and business opportunities that are outside of my area of expertise. While some of these offers are undoubtedly profitable, I have learned to prioritize my focus on my core businesses: real estate, YouTube, and short-term rentals. If someone presents me with a distressed property, such as an apartment building that is delinquent in their payments, or if I have the chance to purchase multiple properties at a discount from a landlord who is interested in selling, those are the types of opportunities that I specialize in. Being clear on the vision for my brand allows me to quickly determine if a potential investment aligns with my expertise and from there, make a confident decision accordingly. This ability gives me the power to think like a CEO and make strategic choices in my area of expertise while expanding the brand.

Although I may sometimes need to think things over, I rarely spend days pondering on it. I believe in making decisions and sticking with them, even if they may not always be the right ones. This trait is something that people either love or hate about me. Personally, I embrace this quality and love it about myself. I make a decision and stick to it. If something is presented to me, I quickly decide whether I will accept or decline. I usually have a gut feeling and if necessary, I may do some research before making a final decision and moving forward. It is important for me to keep moving and not dwell on offers for too long. Indecisiveness is the downfall of many entrepreneurs, which is why I try to avoid constantly second-guessing myself. I understand the importance of seeking advice and gathering information, but relying too heavily on others' opinions can hinder your ability to make strong, independent decisions.

Make Decisions - Quicker

As a person who once struggled with trusting my decisions, I can easily spot when someone struggles in this area. For example, when a prospective coaching client practically stalks me for mentorship, they finally have my undivided attention, I present the offer, and then they hesitate to make a decision, I know they have a problem making decisions. Of course, they don't come out and say this. They hide behind excuses like, "I need to ask my husband or wife," or "Let me do a bit more research." These stall tactics are really just cover-ups for their decision-making inability. It's imperative to have confidence in your choices and trust in your abilities. Don't allow the fear of making the wrong choice to cause you to take advice from your mother, friend, or someone who lacks the expertise to help you make a sound decision. Consequently, for many, a year later, they remain in the same position as before, without progress. The capability to decide, especially when the decision will only better your life, is a crucial one. Let me add this, there is no such thing as a bad investment in yourself. This is what makes CEOs valuable and highly compensated.

Making decisions is empowering, especially when you have confidence in your abilities and have used positive affirmations and self-talk to guide your decision-making process. "When looking at the information gathered from over 25,000 men and women who had experienced failure, lack of decision was almost top of the list of the 30 major causes."[8] To conquer this area, I would suggest you start by taking small steps. Did you know that you can train your brain to make decisions faster? That's right, so go ahead and start taking action on this today.

PICK A HORSE

Begin with something as simple as deciding what you want to eat for dinner. When you are faced with minor choices such as whether to tackle the dishes, reply to an email, or exercise, limit yourself to a quick decision within 30 seconds. For more significant decisions that typically require days or weeks of consideration like where you may want to travel for your next vacation, set a deadline of 30 minutes or by the end of the workday to finalize your choice. Trust your gut and move on with that. Don't overcomplicate it and linger longer than you should. Gather your information, do your due diligence, and make a decision. Next, implement that decision; it's really that simple. Then move on to bigger things.

> **It's estimated that the average adult makes about 35,000 remotely conscious decisions each day."** [9]

While decision-making may come more naturally to some, the skill of making choices is something that can be developed by everyone. Techniques such as narrowing down options, releasing judgment, and practicing mindfulness are methods you can focus on to enhance your decision-making abilities. This is what I love about the

PICK YOUR HORSE AND REIN IT IN

power to choose you. At any time, you can change your indecisive behavior. But, before you do that, you'll need to know why you are indecisive to begin with. Once you attack the root of the problem, you can start combatting it with positive reinforcements.

Reflect and answer these questions.

Do you struggle with needing the validation of others?

Do you have low self-esteem?

Do you believe you are capable of achieving great things?

Do you believe in your ability as a leader?

If you struggle in any of these areas, this can be the reason why you may not feel comfortable with making decisions. Perhaps there is a spouse or parent who is always critical of you, or you have experienced public shame. I share my vulnerable story of losing everything to help you understand that loss and failure is often part of the process. However, failing is no excuse for you to stay there. From today, make a decision to address the insecurities that cause you to question your decisions. Not dealing with the root of the problem will cause your wealth to become delayed.

Indecision is a money blocker. Other money blockers include procrastination, overthinking, doubting yourself, and being overly critical of yourself. All of these are inhibitors to your decision-making ability. I often teach money is energy. It's important to know what attracts it and what repels it when you are building wealth. Energy is neither good nor bad—it just is. Think about this from your perspective. Would you prefer to surround yourself with someone who knows their worth or someone who struggles with liking themselves? Now think about money—do you think money will be drawn to that type of energy? Or do you think money is attracted to confident, self-assured energy?

Just like how a skilled plumber tackles blockages in pipes, you have the power to address and overcome any obstacles that are blocking your progress. By taking on the role of a plumber in your life, you can identify and clear out any money blockers that may be impeding your success. Whether it's limiting beliefs, negative thoughts, unhealthy financial habits, or lack of confidence, you have the ability to unclog these barriers.

Stop Trying to Be Perfect!

Another valuable lesson my mentor taught me was, that done is better than perfect. Trying to be perfect will limit you from making decisions. Don't allow yourself to fall into the trap of feeling pressured to make the "perfect" choice or wait until you feel everything is perfect before you step out. I see this more often in the world of entrepreneurship. I have encountered individuals who are more articulate and charismatic than I am, yet they hesitate to launch their YouTube and social media channels due to their obsession with perfecting every detail. I have fully embraced the mantra that "done is better than perfect." This mindset has been integral to the success of my YouTube channel and social media presence. Rather than fixating on flaws like lipstick smudges or minor errors in my content, I prioritize completion and delivery.

Even in renowned publications with ten million copies sold, I've come across typos, reinforcing the notion that perfection is not the ultimate objective. By valuing progress over perfection, I've been able to consistently produce content and engage with my audience, a principle that has propelled my success in the digital realm. Indecision often arises from a fear of making mistakes and facing the potential consequences of those errors. Are you stuck in a cycle of analysis paralysis? This fear of imperfection will hinder you tremendously.

Choose You and Stand Firm

You must be willing to take risks and overcome your inner struggles. It is common to experience self-consciousness, low confidence, and indecisiveness when starting a business. However, in order to grow as a person and as a business owner, you should face these challenges head-on. Seeking guidance from a coach or mentor can provide the necessary support to take risks, make decisions, and improve oneself. You must overcome the fear of loss and failure in your journey of entrepreneurship. It is important to work on oneself and become stronger in order to achieve success.

It can sometimes be challenging to attract a customer base or substantial following, but it can be done if you are confident and consistent. One of the reasons why I have garnered a significant number of followers on platforms like YouTube and TikTok is because of my clarity and steadfastness in what I do and how I do it. I communicate my message directly and unambiguously. However, it is not just about my excellent communication skills but also my resolute decision-making. I made a definitive choice to focus on real estate. I began by flipping and fixing houses, and obtaining rental properties, and eventually, I decided to teach others. This led me to write books, start a YouTube channel, share my expertise on social media, and create a coaching program that focuses on real estate investing and business. Therefore, when offered opportunities outside of my niche, such as clothing lines, perfumes, or oil and gas investments, I can easily decline.

Being decisive and standing firmly behind your choices are qualities of a strong leader. This confidence is developed by the methods discussed earlier—having peace with your inner self and faith in your abilities. People tend to gravitate towards individuals who exhibit these traits. Don't think this is something you can skip over. As you elevate and progress, you want to be mindful of how you communicate with yourself. Encouraging self-talk will help you cultivate confidence and reinforce your ability to make sound decisions. Conversely, if you lack confidence, seek validation from others, and hesitate to make decisions, it's difficult to be seen as a true leader.

PICK A HORSE

While seeking other people's opinions and asking for help from those who are experienced in your field can be helpful, ultimately, the responsibility lies with you to make the final call. Indecisiveness can lead to an unsuccessful business as clients may hesitate to accept your offers, always thinking they need more information. This creates negative karma in your business. On the other hand, being a decisive person who sticks by their word and decisions creates positive karma, which will benefit your business. This was a valuable lesson I learned on my journey to becoming a great entrepreneur.

Entrepreneurship will not only make you wealthy, but it is the biggest self-development class you will ever enroll in. It will cause you to explore every area of your life. Ultimately, when you hold yourself accountable and undertake a transformation of your entire mindset, the results will be a re-invention of yourself. When I asked my great-aunt for financial assistance, she did not hesitate to decline. I now understand the importance of making firm decisions like she did. I also understand that before you should ask anyone to invest in you, you should first make the investments in yourself. If you don't elevate and grow in the area of personal development, you will find that any monetary investment won't last.

All Hustle and Grind

The longer I am engaged in the world of entrepreneurship, the more I encounter coaches and leaders entering the marketplace encouraging entrepreneurs to become slaves to their business. Well, they aren't using those words exactly, but they are selling the grind and hustle doctrine. Often when people think about leading a financially free life, they believe they will need to sell their firstborn to achieve success. Yes, hard work is crucial for success, but it is not the only factor at play. Contrary to popular belief, achieving success does not necessarily require sacrificing sleep, exercise, or personal well-being. While I agree that it will require sacrifice to reap the rewards, I don't believe you have to lose your family or your sanity in the process. Your ultimate goal should not just be about making money for the sake of it, but about your legacy. You want to be in a position to gain the freedom to control your time, choose your activities, and select your partnerships. In other words, you get to decide the type of life you want.

Entrepreneurship is sometimes clouded by misconceptions, particularly the glorification of the hustle culture. Success is not solely achieved through relentless grind and no sleep. In reality, many individuals who toil the hardest often find themselves struggling financially.

In due time, their physical body and mind will eventually reveal their humanity. We aren't machines, we weren't created to handle an overload of stress for long periods. While work is a necessary part of life, it should not consume every waking moment, as our purpose on this planet extends beyond merely paying bills. On the contrary, our existence is meant to be a journey of purpose, enjoyment, love, and contribution to others. True happiness lies in embracing these values, not in enduring extreme hardships and sacrifices as some narratives suggest. While stories of overcoming adversity are inspiring, it is vital not to internalize the misconception that suffering is a mandatory part of the success story. By recognizing and embracing opportunities for growth and advancement, you can embark on your journey from a place of empowerment and possibility.

Building a thriving business should be done through inspiration, creating efficient systems, and maintaining a healthy work-life balance without the need for excessive grinding or constant exhaustion. The vision you have for your life should determine how you live your life. When I left corporate America, I vowed to spend more time with my children. I didn't want to miss another milestone in their life because I was too busy. What important areas are you sacrificing in your life? What hobbies have you stopped doing because you're too busy? Are you taking the proper time to refuel your body, mind, and soul? Go ahead and decide that things will be different now.

Chapter Review

O History has shown us time and time again that focusing on a singular goal and seeing it through to fruition is a key ingredient to achieving business success.

O The idea of choosing your horse is to choose something you enjoy that simultaneously makes a lot of money; something you will stick to.

O Visionaries understand if they have too many things going on at once, it's like trying to ride multiple horses at one time—it can't be done.

O Successful CEOs are decisive. They don't waver in their choices. They are known for making important decisions that can either make or break a company.

O Trying to be perfect will limit you from making decisions. Don't allow yourself to fall into the trap of feeling pressured to make the "perfect" choice or wait until you feel everything is perfect before you step out.

PICK A HORSE

○ Our existence is meant to be a journey of purpose, enjoyment, love, and contribution to others.

PICK YOUR HORSE AND REIN IT IN

Discover Yourself Now!

SCAN HERE

Pick Your Horse Quiz

NoelleRandall.com/PickYourHorse

CHAPTER FIVE
Choose To Be Great

IN THE EARLY 1960s, Sam Walton, the founder of Walmart had big dreams. He was a visionary who wanted to create something special in the world of retail. He started by opening discount stores in small rural towns, aiming to serve customers who were often overlooked by big retail giants like Sears and Kmart. Sam was clever; he avoided direct competition with these giants and other large department stores, focusing on providing value to those who needed it most.

After seeing success with his dime store, Sam's ambition grew even larger. In 1962, at the age of 44, he opened the very first Walmart in Rogers, Arkansas. Walmart quickly evolved from a simple five-and-dime shop into

CHOOSE TO BE GREAT

a global retail powerhouse by embracing new strategies and principles that set it apart from the rest. They offered over 22 departments selling a variety of products, from shoes to sporting goods. As Walmart grew, it stood out for its unique approach to business. By acquiring small retail businesses and using aggressive pricing strategies, the company rapidly expanded. Sam Walton and his team were always on the lookout for ways to cut costs and improve efficiency. From adopting new technologies to negotiating better deals with suppliers, Walmart constantly innovated to streamline its operations and protect its profits. This dedication to excellence and innovation would set the stage for Walmart to become the retail giant we know today, all starting with one man's vision and a store in a small town in Arkansas.

By the 1990s the company had already solidified its position as one of the biggest retailers in the United States, boasting impressive annual sales that towered over its competitors. With its focus on operational efficiency, utilizing economies of scale, and stringent cost controls, Walmart held a significant edge in the retail landscape. But the story didn't end there; Walmart had grand plans to grow and adapt to the changing times.

As the years passed, Walmart set its sights on international markets, spreading its reach far beyond the borders of the United States. In a remarkable turn of events, by 2001, Walmart's total sales had even surpassed those of Exxon Mobil, propelling it to the coveted title of the largest corporation in the world. It's no secret that Walmart stands as a giant in the retail world. With an impressive network of 10,623 stores and 380 distribution facilities spanning 27 countries, Walmart's annual revenues now soar above $600 billion. A significant portion of its revenue flows in from in-store grocery purchases, highlighting its continued relevance and dominance in the industry.

Think Big!

Are your dreams so big that they scare you? If they don't, you aren't dreaming big enough. Even if you're a small business owner, the goal shouldn't be to remain small. Often people start their business with a small mindset; I believe this is because their vision is limited and they have not been exposed to what is truly possible. This can be attributed to anything from being in a non-supportive environment, or not being exposed to the right information. Every business, no matter where they begin, should be focused on growth. When I mention growth, I am not just focusing on monetary growth. This also includes personal development, skill enhancement, and overall business sustainability. By embracing a mindset geared towards holistic growth, you can unlock your full potential and create a lasting impact in your industry and beyond. I mentioned earlier how my vision expanded when I stepped into the room with real estate investors who had bigger visions. Any entrepreneur that thinks about having a business should be thinking big. I don't want you to limit yourself to making only $3,000 or $4,000 per month in your business. That's fine when you first start, but that should not be where you should aim to stay. While you may be small today, think about how you can grow and expand in the future. You must be willing to grow in your education, your sphere of influence, and your environment.

Implementing a "think big" mindset in business will lead to innovative ideas and success. You do this by setting ambitious goals, challenging the status quo, and pushing the boundaries of what is possible. Often, we place constraints on our own potential. Many people tend to set their sights too low instead of reaching for the stars. It is said that Sam Walton, from a young age, had grand dreams. As he achieved success, his self-belief expanded, and his aspirations soared to new heights. He refused to confine himself to anyone else's boundaries and limitations.

PICK A HORSE

Thinking big allows you to anticipate future trends and opportunities. It helps you stay ahead of the competition and adapt to changes in the market. Building a successful business takes time and effort. Success doesn't happen overnight. You must be willing to put in the work, continuously improve your skills, and stay committed to your goals. With this mindset, you are more likely to take calculated risks that can lead to significant growth for your business. Overall, thinking big is essential for driving innovation, staying competitive, and achieving long-term success.

Walmart was not built in one day. On average, it costs about $14-$22 million to transform an empty field into a 185,000-square-foot building. There is a series of planning, blueprints, building, hiring, product ordering, and everything else that is needed for the grand opening. Each one starts the same. It starts with the vision. It all comes down to the visionary's approach of creating these stores from scratch and conceptualizing the store layout. We shop at a super-Walmart in its completed state but consider this: there are visionaries responsible for designing the shopping carts, parking areas, signage, lighting, employee uniforms, and registers, choosing product vendors, and determining the language and etiquette to be followed by the staff. Every detail counts towards the overall success of the brand.

CHOOSE TO BE GREAT

Walmart's vision includes determining how many registers they can place at the front of their stores and how to maximize the number of checkout stations. This is to ensure that they can process as many transactions as possible per second. This emphasis on efficiency and speed is crucial to the success of the company. Now, can you see why Walmart is willing to invest millions of dollars into its opening operations? The vision of one man, today, serves more than 37 million customers every day and more than 230 million customers every week.

Yes, Walmart is a big business. However, it's not too big for someone like you to achieve. Can you imagine building something that big for you and your family? We all have the power to dream and execute on this level. This is not just reserved for big-box stores, banks, or large corporations. Everything starts with the power of one. Every single business is created like this. From a gym to an apartment complex, to oil refineries, it all starts in the mind of the visionary. Can you look at other big businesses and see yourself operating something of that impact and magnitude? In order to create something great, it starts with your vision.

Become a Visionary

Can you see 'it' before everyone else believes in you? Being a visionary and being able to visualize are key components of having a successful big business. Your vision is the foundational piece. Visualization is probably not an unfamiliar word to you. It's often used in personal development, yoga and mantras, and other spaces. Visualization is a powerful mind tool and exercise for realizing your aspirations and accomplishing your objectives. Like exercise, your visualization muscle gets stronger the more you do it; it works by preparing your mind and body for what you want to happen. Take time daily to visualize your success. The first person that you must convince of your great vision is yourself. Once you can accept that you are worthy of wealth, you can begin to build it.

Think about your legacy. Let your mind expand. Your vision should be as big as you can imagine. There's no reason to think small. You only get one life. We're here on this earth for one time and then we will not be here anymore. There are no do-overs and there's no point in safely tiptoeing our way to death. You need to think big. Consider the future of your company. What will your business look like 10 years from now? What about 20 to 30 years from now? This is the starting point of any business idea. Don't allow this process to overwhelm you. You don't have to have it all figured out right now, you just need to be open to the big possibilities. Keep the idea in mind that you are building something big.

Evolving into a Visionary

To build a thriving business, several essential components must be considered. The first of these is vision. According to the Oxford Dictionary, "A vision is the ability to think about or plan the future with imagination or wisdom." Additionally, a visionary has strong, original ideas about how things might be different in the future and is willing to build on this. Becoming a visionary entails self-reflection, a vision statement, implementation, motivation and consistency, and honesty.

> **#1) Self-reflection**: This is a powerful tool that connects you to your purpose. It also helps you adapt to challenges and continue growing personally and professionally in your journey. Take some time to reflect on your values, passions, strengths, and aspirations. Consider what truly matters to you and what you want to achieve in different areas of your life, such as finances, relationships, health, and personal development and growth.

PICK A HORSE

My vision for my life:

Financial:

Relationships:

Health:

Personal Development and Growth:

#2) Vision statement: A vision statement is a guide for what you see for your future. If you don't have one already, create a short and powerful vision statement that sums up your dreams and goals in life. Let it be inspiring, easy to understand, and a true reflection of what matters most to you. If you have written one previously, this is a good time to read it again to make sure your focus hasn't changed. You'll probably notice that as your exposure expands, so will your vision.

Reflect on your life vision statement.

#3) **Implementation**: Implementation refers to the process of putting a plan or decision into effect. It is the practical, step-by-step process of achieving maximum results. This involves doing what is necessary to manifest an idea, design, or concept into reality. Implementation is the doing of the idea. An idea is absolutely nothing if it's never implemented or if action is never taken. To implement a vision successfully, it is crucial to communicate it effectively, build a team that is aligned with the vision, and empower them to take ownership of their roles in achieving the shared goal. It also entails adapting to changes, overcoming obstacles, and staying focused. Implementation is about taking the first steps. It's about taking risks.

#4) **Motivation and Consistency**: Stay motivated and revisit your vision regularly. Keep your vision statement somewhere visible to remind yourself of your goals. Stay motivated by celebrating small victories along the way, and regularly revisit and revise your vision as you grow and evolve. Show up every day ready to take another step towards your goals.

#5) Honesty: To be a visionary, you must be very honest, especially with yourself. Embracing a growth mindset, being receptive to guidance, and working on your areas of weakness will greatly enhance your chances of succeeding as a business visionary.

Successful Habits for Building Wealth

Assess Your Behavior and Patterns

Our habits and behaviors are key factors in determining the levels of success we reach. When was the last time you asked yourself "why" as it relates to your habits? Why do I do that? Why do I need coffee every morning? Why do I crave sugar at the same time every day? Why do I feel the need to exaggerate how much I have, where I've been, or who I know? If you don't take the time to ask yourself why or notate your behaviors, it will be a long hard road to success. I would even go on further and say you will probably never reach true success. Our behaviors—both positive and negative—have a tremendous impact on our lives.

This is a good time for you to take an assessment of your patterns and behaviors. Ask yourself, if I continue to repeat these behaviors, will they lead to the greatest version of myself? Do your daily routines indicate you are on the path to becoming wealthy? Do you pay attention to what you spend and what you earn? Does your daily routine include more activities that help you to build wealth or subtract from you? Are you still trying to keep up with the last Netflix release or are you spending more time studying your craft? Do you wake up by a certain time or do you sleep in late? Many CEOs start their day early, often waking up before the sun rises to get a head start on their tasks. They prioritize activities like exercise, meditation, or reading to sharpen their minds and bodies for the day ahead. Studies on successful CEOs consistently highlight how they guard their time because they realize this is the only thing in life that cannot be replaced or recreated. You can lose money and earn it back, but you can never gain back your time. Successful people understand this and are particular about using their time wisely. They schedule their days and accomplish more because they don't allow every person or problem to deplete them. They are deliberate and intentional.

When you think about your days, are they structured and planned, or do you go along with the flow—allowing others to dictate how you use your time? Setting clear goals and planning their day meticulously are other common practices among successful CEOs enabling them to stay focused and productive. People often wonder how I am able to achieve what I have—being a mother of young and adult children, a son with autism, and a wife. The answer is simple, I plan my life and include time for the unexpected. I typically awake between the hours of 4:00 AM and 6:00 AM to start my day. My mentor taught me the importance of waking up before my children to get more accomplished. This practice has allowed me to become more productive as well as feel more in control of my day. This practice has consistently worked for me and my family. In fact, it is so routine that I also see my children waking up earlier for high school and college to allow themselves time to get in the best mind space to start their day.

Take Accountability and Responsibility

Accountability is another important trait that successful CEOs have in common. They understand the importance of holding themselves and their teams accountable for their actions and decisions. By setting high standards and taking ownership of both successes and failures, CEOs create a culture of responsibility within their organizations. This fosters a sense of trust and transparency, leading to improved performance and teamwork.

When leaders take responsibility for the success or lack of, they express their ability to lead. Instead of blaming external factors for setbacks, successful CEOs analyze the situation, learn from their mistakes, and take steps to rectify the issue. By accepting responsibility, they demonstrate leadership qualities that inspire trust and respect among their employees and stakeholders. This proactive approach to problem-solving sets them apart and propels their company forward.

Read, Read, and Keep Reading

Upon joining a mentorship program, the first gift presented to me was a book by John C. Maxwell called *How Successful People Think*. This book was not like any other textbook I had received during my time at the University of Connecticut. It wasn't just a book; it was a tool that provided insight into how to think like a successful person. The fact that my mentor gave me this book as my first gift spoke volumes about the program and what it could offer me. Even to this day, I still refer to it as one of my guiding principles. It's amazing how something as simple as a book can change the way you think and approach life. Throughout the program, a new book arrived every month, as part of the coaching. My coach understood that reading is essential to being a successful leader and that all the necessary information

PICK A HORSE

could be found within a book. However, beyond gaining knowledge, the habit of reading is a priceless characteristic for any individual who aspires to greatness.

The gift of literacy is taken for granted by many people. We often fail to appreciate the immense power and value of being able to read. We learned while studying the history of slavery in the United States, that reading was a forbidden activity. Slave owners believed that education would make slaves difficult to control, and so they prevented them from learning how to read. This lack of education and literacy effectively stripped slaves of their freedom, leaving them at the mercy of their oppressors. As an avid reader, I have come to realize the true value of reading and have made it a priority to read as much as I can. In a single year, I aim to read at least 24 books, averaging two books per month. Sometimes, I even revisit books that I have already read as I believe that the person who reads the book changes, not the book itself.

One such book that has had a profound impact on me is Mark Manson's, *The Subtle Art of Not Giving a F*ck*. When I first read it, my main takeaway was not caring what others think. However, when I read it again after achieving financial success, I gained an even deeper understanding of the book's message. The main lesson I learned from that book is that we can still care about people while disregarding their opinions. This bestselling book is popular because it teaches readers that they cannot give importance to every little thing in life. The author emphasizes the significance of this lesson in various areas of our lives, particularly in our fear of failure and concern for other's opinions. By giving too much importance to such things, we create meanings that could hinder our personal growth. Some of the most dangerous phrases in the human language are, "What will other people say?" and "What will other people think?" To gain knowledge and overcome these fears, reading books is an excellent tool.

There are many books that can help you open up and become more courageous, such as *The Courage to Be Disliked: The Japanese Phenomenon That Shows You How to Change Your Life and Achieve Real Happiness* by authors Ichiro Kishimi and Fumitake Koga and *It Takes What It Takes: How to Think Neutrally and Gain Control of Your Life* by authors Trevor Moawad and Andy Staples. When I first launched my real estate business, I also read books on sales by Zig Ziglar and Joe Gerard. Other books like, *Think and Grow Rich* by Napoleon Hill is another informative read. It provides insights into autosuggestion, repetition, visualization, and the power of connecting with other like-minded individuals. Similarly, *Atomic Habits: An Easy & Proven Way to*

PICK A HORSE

Build Good Habits & Break Bad Ones by James Clear, is another helpful book that offers valuable lessons for personal growth and development. By reading and applying the principles from these books, you can develop new habits and achieve your goals.

As an avid reader, I have found that certain books have had a profound impact on my personal and professional growth. *The Richest Man in Babylon* by George S. Clason and *Secrets of the Millionaire Mind: Mastering the Inner Game of Wealth* by T. Harv Eker were among the first books that I read repeatedly. As I grew older, I began to explore the works of different authors such as Dr. Joe Dispenza's *Becoming Supernatural: How Common People Are Doing the Uncommon*. Recently I read, *The Diary of a CEO: The 33 Laws of Business and Life* by Steven Bartlett, which provided insights on building a successful business doing what you love.

Reading not only provides valuable information, but it also inspires action. While reading is a great skill set, it is important to take action and apply what you learn to see real results. By developing a habit of seeking knowledge, you can differentiate yourself from others and gain access to skills and abilities that others may lack. Although I don't consider myself to be smarter than others, I have an insatiable appetite for information and can consume it efficiently. Reading is a gift that we all possess, and developing this skill can lead to great success.

I was fortunate to have a mentor who taught me that readers are leaders. I embraced this message and realized that knowledge of the world is in books. If you read books, you become powerful. It's important to remember that people who don't want others to have power often prevent them from reading. If you want to reach the next level in your life, reading is crucial. But it's not enough to simply read—you must also implement what you learn and take action. There is a difference between being in motion and being in action. Reading is a valuable tool for personal growth and development.

Health and Wellness

> **"** Hard work is not the path to Well-being. Feeling good is the path to Well-being. You don't create through action; you create through vibration. And then, your vibration calls action from you."
>
> Abraham Hicks

As an entrepreneur, prioritizing your wellness journey is mandatory. Unlike traditional workplaces where mental health days are sometimes offered, as a business owner, you are in charge of your own well-being. Customers aren't going to ask you to take time off. No one is going to tell you to take a break, eat lunch, or take a vacation. You are in charge of your mental and emotional well-being. So, what does this mean? This means that you should schedule time away to refuel. You will be responsible for putting a vacation on your calendar. You will need to schedule date nights, family dinners, and whatever else that helps you stay grounded such as spa days, girls or guy trips, weekend getaways, or staycations. And while we're on this topic—let's also normalize taking the time to celebrate a win, a new contract, and your work anniversary.

I will always be your biggest advocate for taking the time you need to be human.

These are the discussions that are somehow left out of the masterminds and boardrooms. It's essential not to fall into the trap of solely chasing money, that you forget about the freedom you want. Isn't this why we want to become financially free? Isn't *free*-dom what many of us are truly seeking? Well, if freedom is what you want, then don't build a life that keeps you enslaved. Be careful not to create a "team no-sleep" mantra in your business. You need your sleep! By maintaining a clear and healthy mental state, you can cultivate a positive environment that naturally attracts prosperity towards you. Remember, your well-being is the foundation upon which your business success is built, so investing in self-care and mindfulness is key to achieving sustainable growth and happiness in your entrepreneurial endeavors.

Mental health and wellness for an entrepreneur are essential aspects that can significantly impact their success and overall well-being. As an entrepreneur, managing stress, maintaining a work-life balance, and seeking support when needed are key components of mental wellness. Setting boundaries, practicing self-care, and taking breaks are essential to prevent burnout and maintain a healthy mindset. Additionally, staying organized, prioritizing tasks, and delegating responsibilities can help you reduce feelings of overwhelm and anxiety.

Ultimately, mental health and wellness for an entrepreneur involve self-awareness, proactive steps to manage stress, and a commitment to prioritizing mental well-being. Taking care of your mental health enhances your productivity, creativity, and overall satisfaction in both your personal and professional lives. It also makes you likeable by the people you work with and those that hire you. When you are internally peaceful, rested, and healthy, your energy will reflect this.

Hire a Coach!

If you are uncertain about how to achieve the success you desire, seeking the help of a coach might be a pivotal move toward your goals. A coach provides essential guidance, knowledge, and organized support to assist you in achieving success. A coach can inspire you to overcome problems, harness your strengths, and unlock your full potential via individualized tactics, feedback, and responsibility. Collaborating with a coach can provide you with clarity, concentration, and the essential tools to advance toward the success you imagine.

Choose Greatness!

Greatness is a choice, and you hold the key to your destiny. The power to determine the extent of success, the level of prosperity, and the overall quality of life rests firmly in your hand. Regardless of your background or circumstances, we all have equal access to the opportunity to shape our futures through the choices we make. As you reflect on the profound impact of this realization, take hold of the reins of your life with confidence and determination, knowing that greatness truly is within your reach.

Those who achieve greatness are often characterized by their ability to adapt to change and remain resilient in the face of adversity. They are flexible in their approach, open to new ideas, and quick to pivot when circumstances demand it. Average people, on the other hand, may struggle to adapt to change and may become easily discouraged when faced with obstacles.

Are You Ready to Embrace Greatness?

What is your definition of greatness?

Think about someone (living, or not) that you consider to be great. What characteristics do they have that you admire?

What do you feel separates average people from great people?

PICK A HORSE

Do you have a fear of becoming great? Why or why not?

It is often said greatness is learned; do you believe this? Why or why not?

Chapter Review

- By embracing a mindset geared towards holistic growth, you can unlock your full potential and create a lasting impact in your industry and beyond.

- Thinking big allows you to anticipate future trends and opportunities. It helps you stay ahead of the competition and adapt to changes in the market.

- Being a visionary and being able to visualize are key components of having a successful big business.

- Becoming a visionary entails self-reflection, a vision statement, implementation, motivation and consistency, and honesty.

- By maintaining a clear and healthy mental state, you can cultivate a positive environment that naturally attracts prosperity towards you.

- Those who achieve greatness are often characterized by their ability to adapt to change and remain resilient in the face of adversity.

CHAPTER SIX

What Will It Take to Achieve Your Success?

In 2007, while attending a university in Perth, Australia, 26-year-old Melanie Perkins had a crazy big idea. While working a part-time job teaching students to use desktop design software, programs that were hard to learn and expensive to buy, she wanted to build an online tool that would empower anyone to create great designs regardless of their experience. Her idea was Canva. You may be familiar with the name. It is the company that has taken the graphic design world by storm. In an interview about her story, Melanie mentions that after a chance meeting with Bill Tai, a legendary venture capitalist from Silicon Valley, she was invited to make her first pitch. Despite her initial reservations, she accepted an invitation to meet him in San Francisco. That impressed him enough to introduce her to others and invite her to his unique retreat for investors and kitesurfing enthusiasts, Mai Tai.

"So, every time he would say, 'How was my business going?' he'd also be like, 'How's your kitesurfing going?' So, I kind of needed to learn to kitesurf. I had not done it before. And, to be honest, it's not something that I would normally, naturally try. But yeah, decided to give it a go because when you don't have any connections, you don't have any network, you just kind of have to wedge your foot in the door and wiggle it all the way through." shares Melanie during an interview.[10]

Three years into her pitching process, with over 100 rejections later, Canva received its first investment of $3 million in seed funding. Today, Canva, the online design firm, is now valued at $40 billion. That makes Canva one of the world's most valuable female-founded and female-led startups.[11] What she has built along with her co-founders is impressive, however, there is something that stands out even more. Before meeting Mr. Tai, she had never kite-surfed, and I will bet that it was never on her bucket list. To get in front of the right room and close the deal, she was faced with a choice. She could have either declined because she had no idea about the watersport or chose the route of learning the sport. Obviously, she chose the latter; but why? It's because when you believe in something so badly and the access to what you want is on the other side—you can't let anything stand in your way. Even if it means learning a sport you have no idea about, if making that move will put you in the right environment—it's worth it. Learning more about Melanie, even surviving the ridicule she received after the initial launch of the product; the fact that she still managed to rise and become a billionaire shows the power and persistence of an entrepreneur.

Run Towards the Roar

When you are ready to experience that next level, take advantage of the opportunities that place you out of your comfort zone and allow you to enter new rooms. Well, in my world—new greens. I remember my chance encounter during a mentorship program that changed my perspective entirely about golf. A mentor, not directly affiliated with me but whose speech I attended, shared an intriguing insight. He suggested that taking up the sport of golf could be a strategic move in the world of business, particularly as I wanted to grow my real estate investment portfolio. He stated and I quote "You want to make a million dollars? Buy a Bentley, head to the golf course, and tell people you are in real estate. You'll make out with a lot of deals because they'll see you as wealthy." I initially laughed when I heard it. Back then, the idea seemed far-fetched; I didn't know anything about golf and I couldn't afford to drive a Bentley. I later learned he was on to something.

As a Caribbean, African American woman in my 30s, diving into the world of golf was never something I saw on my horizon. Initially, stepping onto the golf course felt like venturing into uncharted territory. The intimidation factor was palpable at the start. I was a novice among seasoned players, many of whom had been perfecting their swing since childhood. The golf course was their domain, and I, with my hesitant strokes and unfamiliarity with the sport's nuances, felt conspicuously out of place. The sport is predominantly played by many individuals who don't look like me—mostly males, and few, if any, are African American or of Caribbean descent. Not only did I feel out of my league, but the sport also wasn't easy to learn. I remember how dull of a sport it was as I struggled to hit the ball and learn the terminology.

Challenging myself to show up consistently although I often felt awkward, reminds me of a powerful motivational lesson I heard titled "Run to the Roar." It tells the story of how the old lion, unable to hunt, uses its roar to scare prey towards the waiting pack of younger, able lions. Even in their old age, when lions lose their teeth and can no longer engage in hunting or attacking, their roar remains potent. Interestingly, these elder lions hold a distinguished status within the pride. The pride cleverly uses an aged lion, placing it close to potential prey, relying on its intimidating roar to drive the prey directly into the path of the younger, more agile lions poised for the kill. Remarkably, these younger lions remain silent during the hunt, opting for a stealthy approach rather than roaring. This strategic use of the elder lion's roar in the hunting process is a captivating aspect of lion behavior. This story taught me that we need to run towards the things that scare us, not away from them. By facing my fears and stepping into the intimidating world of golf, I wasn't just learning a sport; I was running towards my roar.

Golf turned out to be the exact challenge I needed. It wasn't about physical speed or athleticism, qualities I had relied on as a track runner in high school and college. Instead, golf demanded skill, mindset, and concentration — aspects that were crucial for my growth in business. It taught me how to maintain confidence and hold my own in rooms filled with individuals far wealthier and more experienced than me. Stepping onto the golf course was like stepping into a new realm, one where I learned to master a new skill set and, in turn, elevate my business to new heights.

Today, I have surprised not only myself but many others with my newfound passion for the sport. I've fully immersed myself in the golfing world, complete with my very own set of clubs and a membership at the local Country Club. It's become a part of my routine, visiting the club at least a couple of times a month, and at one point, I was there every single week, swinging away with fervor. I don't pull up driving a Bentley to the golf course, but I do drive up in my Lamborghini, a testament to how far I've come. When I share with fellow golfers that I'm in real estate, doors beyond my wildest imagination have opened for me. My golfing skills may still be a work in progress, but I've come to understand and appreciate the game's intricacies, from the lingo and etiquette to the attire. More importantly, golf has become more than just a hobby—it's a networking platform, a space where I've defied expectations and stereotypes, and where I've found unexpected opportunities to grow professionally and personally. I have discovered a world that is filled with successful individuals, from doctors to real estate moguls and hotel owners, each carrying a wealth of knowledge and connections. The more I opened myself up to this new world, the more doors opened for me. Friends introduced me to their accountants, lawyers, and other key contacts, expanding my network and resources in ways I never imagined.

This journey towards the roar not only transformed my business but also reshaped my approach to challenges, making me realize that sometimes, the path to greatness requires us to face our fears head-on. I used to see the world of people as an intimidating space, always feeling a bit out of place and hesitant to mingle. Yet, deep down, I knew that stepping into those circles, embracing the unknown, and being willing to stand out were the keys to unlocking opportunities and breakthroughs. To make significant strides, you will need to embrace your challenges and excel. It was in this spirit that I ventured into the world of golf. When you are undoubtedly ready for the freedom you are seeking, you will need to evolve. You will need to challenge yourself to connect with people who don't look like you or run in your circle of friends. My journey into golf was not just about picking up a new hobby; it was about immersing myself in an environment that was once foreign and intimidating to me.

In the previous chapter, we discussed thinking big like the CEO that you are. So, now, let's take this a step further to experience success. Remember what I mentioned in the introduction of this book? I want you to learn how to be a doer. The world is filled with consumers of knowledge, but not so many doers. Take a moment to visualize what success looks like to you. Reflect on what it will take for you to build something so amazing that people will be writing about you for years to come. What type of focus and determination will be required for you to achieve your definition of success? What new challenge do you need to take on that will put you in the right environment? Maybe kite-surfing or golfing isn't something you are interested in. But where can you meet people ready to do business with you? Where can you connect with others who want the products or services that you offer and can pay you well for the value you bring them? Success leaves clues.

The Success Blueprint

I: Pick a Horse

We detailed this subject extensively in Chapter 4. By now you should know what your focus will be. I will add one more tip here. Start with something you have knowledge of already. Don't try and re-invent the wheel or delay the launch. Consider leveraging your existing knowledge to not only give you a solid starting point but also to instill confidence as you progress. This approach allows you to navigate through your business with a sense of familiarity, making the process less daunting.

II: Write the Plan

Developing both life and wealth plans are important steps toward achieving your goals and realizing your full potential. To begin, set clear and specific goals that are both demanding and realistic. An unwritten plan is no plan at all. Once you have written your plan, review it often.

III: Create the Process and System to Produce the Results

Our world and life exist and thrive because of systems. Everything that is successful has a process with a defined system behind it. Our bodies have systems—some of those systems include the muscular, nervous, cardiovascular, lymphatic, respiratory, and digestive. Think about how important your respiratory system is. Its main function is to move fresh air into your body while removing waste gases. What would happen if that system stopped working properly? If left untreated, respiratory failure can cause serious complications such as organ damage due to lack of oxygen, respiratory arrest, and even death.

This is how important systems are to your organization. There is a process to achieving what you want. Failure to implement business systems will lead to the demise of your company. Those who understand this are the people who take control of their day, time, and resources instead of going whichever path the wind blows them. The visionary details how each department of their business will function. The mistake I see many entrepreneurs make is they have no systems in place, making it difficult to scale and build. It's like tossing a bowl of spaghetti towards the ceiling and hoping that it will stick. They don't take the time to slow down to understand the process. I am constantly conducting audits in my business. I review key performance indicators (KPIs) and adjust the process accordingly. This involves taking the time to learn from each customer. I study what makes them buy and what causes them to hesitate to buy.

As you begin to build more in your business, you will continuously tweak your process until you find what works. Make sure you also document how you did it. How long does it take to complete a task? What are the required steps? What software did you use? What questions did you ask the prospect during the sales consultation? Once you understand what works, it makes it so much easier to hire others and scale. When you understand every aspect of your business, you can seamlessly train your

PICK A HORSE

hires to help you build faster and more efficiently. Think about how much more efficient you can become when you don't have to personally train each new hire because you have a manual and/ or training videos. How much more efficient can you become if you don't need to speak directly to each prospect because your team has a discovery call script? How much more will your business grow when you don't have to send invoices and track down each payment? Yes, you may start there but remember what we discussed in Chapter 5 about big businesses. Although you may be small now, you will grow.

It is my suggestion that you have systems in place for each area of your business. These include sales, marketing, customers, finance, employees, products and/or services, technology, contracts and legal. At minimum, your systems should include the total customer experience. If you are in the service industry, this will include every touchpoint from the time you connect with a prospect to the time you off-board them. If you are in the products industry, think about the customers' first exposure to the product and how you can get them to the checkout. Don't forget your team's duties and expectations, timelines, and your profit and loss. You can never have too many systems.

WHAT WILL IT TAKE TO ACHIEVE YOUR SUCCESS?

When creating your systems ask yourself questions to help you formulate the best process. Below are some prompts to help get you started.

How many prospects do we need to speak with to reach the sales goals?

How will we offer top-notch customer service and retain customers?

How much will we charge for products and/or services?

What technology will we need to deliver the products/services?

How will we accept payments for products or services?

What legal team will we retain to create and review contracts?

These are just some of the basic questions that will help you formulate your process. Depending on the type of business and industry you are in, you will need to identify the proper systems to help you operate more efficiently.

IV: Create a Checkpoint System

Once you create the system, next implement your trial-and-error checkpoint to ensure that the system works and creates the results you need. Perhaps what you thought was a good practice for customers is now resulting in a high turnover. This is a sign that something needs to be adjusted for better results. Documenting the system allows you to review the steps to assess where the breakdown in the system occurred. It also helps you to become more organized. Efficiency is important in the life of an entrepreneur. As you implement systems and document the process, you will learn from each client, each transaction, and each interaction.

V: Have a Growth Plan and Strategy

When you assess your growth plan, also evaluate your growth and/or decline in customers. Do you know that having more customers doesn't always equate to growth? That's right! In certain circumstances, having more clients indicate growth, while in other cases, having fewer clients that pay more can also indicate growth. The essential thing is to create a business model that works best for you. Ultimately you want to grow and improve by delivering better results to your customers. The pulse of your business will be evident in the sustainability of your processes. As you are building you should always have a growth plan.

To achieve success, it's vital to understand the principle of "grow or die." This principle mirrors human life, where we continuously evolve and grow; otherwise, we risk stagnation and decline. Every business should aim for growth and development, and this growth is not limited to an increase in customer base or revenue. It can manifest in an enhancement of the quality of services provided or the ability to attract and retain clients. Growth can also mean the development of systems that are in place and/or the growth of the business's leaders. To ensure continued success, it's essential for any business to assess regularly what's working and what's not,

PICK A HORSE

and strive towards growth and development. The key to success is to keep improving the business's ability to deliver positive outcomes.

The reason why we frequently return to shop in stores like Walmart or Target is that they constantly introduce new products, have items that we need, and offer fantastic sales and holiday discounts. These businesses have always grown. Big box retailers like Target and Walmart started with a single store, and now they have multiple locations. Walmart, in particular, has achieved growth over the years by expanding and offering a wide range of services and products including auto centers, grocery stores, nail salons, and banks. Does this growth model work for every type of business? No, it doesn't. Some businesses have tried to enter as a competitor in the big-box market and failed. The key is to find out what works, do more of that, and stop doing the things that don't. This is growth. The primary objective of your business should be to grow, and if you are not, then you are dying.

One of the easiest ways to assess the health of your business is in your business income. If you are not increasing in profits, assess your growth plan. It is essential to track what works and what doesn't in your business and to continue to innovate and launch new products or strategies. While some ideas may not be successful, there is always the potential for a profitable outcome.

There are three primary ways that you can make money in your business.

#1) Secure More Customers:

Think of creative ways to attract and retain more customers. Think about what problems they have and how you can solve them. You can attract customers to your business through the traditional ways of marketing and advertising, but what are some non-traditional ways you can consider? What gaps in the market does your business offer solutions for? Where do your prospects spend their time? Become more visible in those places where your prospects are. There are many ways to connect with potential customers; don't miss the opportunity to let people know about your business. By advertising and marketing effectively, you can reach a wider audience and increase your customer base.

#2) Increase Your Prices:

Another strategy that businesses can use to increase their revenue is to raise their prices. As a company grows and provides more value to its customers, it can justify increasing the prices of its products or services.

#3) **Re-connect with Past Customers**:
You want to encourage repeat customer business. By offering additional products or services and maintaining strong relationships with customers through follow-up emails or phone calls, you can cultivate a loyal customer base. Target is a prime example of a company that has mastered this strategy. They continually adjust their products and pricing and marketing to keep customers returning to spend more money. If you have purchased items from Target, you will automatically begin to receive their email marketing. They aren't shy about contacting you and promoting their next sale. They understand that follow-up after a sale is also crucial, as it provides an opportunity to address any concerns or issues the customer may have had and can help to build trust and loyalty over time. Earlier I encouraged you to think like a big business. Marketing products and services is an area that many big businesses dominate while small businesses are afraid to promote too much.

Your growth plan should also include following up on leads. Create a system in your business to follow up on leads, to close the sale, and even after the sale is completed. This is especially important for a new entrepreneur in business. Follow up on leads that did not convert. Follow up on customers that you served and see what you can do to serve them better. What else can you sell to them in the future? If you own an online business, make sure you become familiar with cart abandonment and email marketing. For example, if a customer places an item in their cart and then abandons it, sending them an email reminder to purchase the item can be an effective way to increase sales. Amazon is a good company to emulate as they use this strategy and track customer behavior across multiple platforms. The advertising feature reminds potential customers of the items they were previously interested in but did not purchase.

VI. Reinvesting in Your Business

Often when a new entrepreneur makes a sale, they immediately spend that money. That's a big mistake. If you want to have a successful business you must resist the urge to spend everything you earn, especially when starting out. To grow, you must continue to plant. The more money you invest back into your business, the more you will see growth. I regretted not reinvesting more money into my business in the initial years, which I believe contributed to the inconsistency of growth and low profit. When I hired a coach, my mentor taught me the importance of re-investment and how to consistently market my business with the correct systems. Acquiring this knowledge proved to be the turning point in my entrepreneurial journey. It is recommended to allocate a portion, around 20-30% of your earnings, back into your business as a means of fostering growth and sustainability. This proactive approach can yield long-term benefits and facilitate the expansion of your enterprise.

VII. Believe in Your Brand

Before you can influence your customers to buy your product or service, you first need to believe in your business. Having unfaltering faith in your business is vital if you want to persuade a potential client to buy your goods or services. Customers are more likely to have faith in your brand when they see that you genuinely believe in the worth and quality of your products and services. Your passion and enthusiasm for your product or service will significantly impact your potential buyer. I believe this is why I have found success on my YouTube channel. I truly believe in my business. I believe in the results we help our students achieve, and I am passionate about helping others. People who tune in can feel my commitment and energy. If you truly believe in what you're selling, you'll be more equipped to persuade potential customers of its value and win over their concerns and objections. Your ability to craft an engaging story that resonates with potential consumers and encourages them to buy is directly correlated to the amount of self-assurance you project.

Achieving success in your business requires structure, organization, planning, and everything else we discussed but most importantly it requires you to have a success mindset. You truly need to believe, above anything else, that you are worthy and deserving of it. You don't need an MBA to be successful in business. Some successful entrepreneurs didn't graduate from high school. According to Guidant Financial, "about 30% of entrepreneurs only finish high school, 31% have an associate degree, 17% have a bachelor's degree, 18% obtained a master's degree, and 4% have a PhD. Formal education can help many career paths but doesn't seem to be very important for entrepreneurship."[12] Success is not solely based on education, but also on confidence and the ability to recognize and use your strengths while aligning yourself with others who excel in areas you may not. We started off this book by expressing the importance of choosing you. When you fully comprehend what this means, you will shift into a growth and wealth magnet. You'll gravitate towards the best practices and attract what you are truly looking for.

Chapter Review

○ Developing a personal success plan is an important step toward achieving your goals and realizing your full potential.

○ Have systems in place for each area of your business. This includes sales, marketing, customers, finance, employees, products and/or services, technology, contracts and legal.

○ Every business should aim for growth and development, and this growth is not limited to an increase in customer base or revenue.

○ The primary objective of your business should be to grow, and if you are not, then you are dying.

○ It is recommended to allocate a portion, around 20-30%, of your earnings back into your business as a means of fostering growth and sustainability.

○ Customers are more likely to have faith in your brand when they see that you genuinely believe in the worth and quality of your products and services.

WHAT WILL IT TAKE TO ACHIEVE YOUR SUCCESS?

Listen, Learn, and Grow

SCAN HERE

Noelle's Podcasts

NoelleRandall.com/Podcasts

CHAPTER SEVEN
Who's Coming With You?

Richard "Billionaire" Branson made a tweet about employees. His message was short, to the point, and yet profound.

> **"Train people well enough so they can leave. Treat them well enough so they don't want to."**[13]

With such an impressive biography, it's probably safe to say he knows a thing or two about building successful teams and being a great leader. He's admired not only for his net worth of an estimated $2.9 billion but also for building businesses that employ 70,000+ employees. His rise to prominence occurred after he founded Virgin Records in 1973. The company became a key player in the punk and new wave music scene globally. From there, he rebranded an airline into Virgin Atlantic Airways showcasing his entrepreneurial spirit, with the company's expansion being fueled by the sale of Virgin Records in 1992. In the early 2000s, the trailblazer launched Virgin Galactic, a space tourism venture aimed at providing commercial suborbital trips for passengers. These days, at the age of 73, he has control of over 400 companies.

I recently learned that Richard Branson, despite being a billionaire, is dyslexic and struggles with reading. This goes to show that one can achieve great success without being good at everything. It shows that great leadership is not about your educational background. In fact, I've met numerous entrepreneurs who have become millionaires and multi-millionaires, without being great students. Instead, they excel at communication and public speaking, and possess a charismatic personality. On the other hand, I have also encountered incredibly smart individuals, with genius-level intellect, who struggle in business and leading others.

Accomplishing great things requires a concerted effort from people working together. When people work

PICK A HORSE

together, they can generate immense power. No matter how amazing of a visionary you are, it's very difficult to build an empire on your own. Achieving great things in business will involve collaboration and teamwork. There is a saying that "like attracts like," and this is essential in building a team, especially when building a big business. It's imperative that you surround yourself with people who share your vision, beliefs, and objectives. The engine that propels creativity, productivity, and expansion is a cohesive team whose members gel nicely. Every member of the team contributes a unique element to the team dynamic and the company's overall performance. Having said that, the company can suffer if the team consists of people who aren't the right fit.

The year my company took its biggest hit financially was when I hired the wrong person to manage the business. It was a very hard and expensive lesson. Hiring someone that is not a right fit for the culture or can't keep up with the demands and leadership required for your company's profitability, is a recipe for disaster. That year, millions of dollars were lost because of mismanagement and their lack of leadership skills. This was a beautifully amazing person and because we had similarities in that we both were moms, ambitious, and from similar backgrounds, I made the mistake of bringing her on. Ultimately, the rise and fall of a company stands on the shoulders of the leadership, however, the team will also be a major factor in its success.

Many lessons were learned after that year. I was forced to take an assessment of my hiring practices and criteria for future hires. I pivoted and implemented the hiring practices I observed while working in corporate. Wells Fargo incorporated the SBO (situation, behavior, outcome) method that was used in interviews to help reveal the authenticity and experience of a candidate's responses. For example, if the candidate was interviewing for a sales position, the interviewer would ask:

Situation: Explain a time when you had to deal with a difficult customer in a previous sales role. How did you handle the situation?

Behavior: Can you provide an example of a time when you had to meet a challenging sales target? What specific actions did you take to exceed expectations?

Outcome: Share a situation where you successfully upsold a product to a customer. What was the outcome of your upselling efforts, and how did it benefit both the customer and the company?

When questions are posed in this manner, it prompts a genuine on-the-spot answer instead of a rehearsed response, which allows for a better assessment of the capabilities and problem-solving skills of the candidate. It is common to encounter rehearsed scenarios during interviews, but this approach aims to differentiate genuine experiences from fabricated stories. By delving into specific instances from a candidate's past, a deeper insight into their problem-solving skills and capabilities can be gained. This method is particularly effective in assessing a candidate's suitability for a position by focusing on their behavior in different situations and the outcomes of those encounters.

Before making a hiring decision, establish the abilities, personality qualities, and temperament required for the position. This clarity lays the groundwork for an effective hiring process. Using behavior-based questions during interviews can assist with properly analyzing candidates and ensuring that their experiences match the requirements of the role. Authenticity shines through when candidates can share tangible instances from previous employment to demonstrate their suitability for the job at hand.

People Follow Great Leadership

Vision, honesty, and empathy are among the traits of a leader that can inspire people to strive for a common objective. Great leaders inspire trust and commitment in their team by leading by example, speaking clearly, and remaining receptive to fresh perspectives. When team members feel heard and valued, they are more likely to be involved, effective, and dedicated to the goal of the company. When they are led by someone they look up to and respect, they show up ready to roll up their sleeves and support the brand. A great leader encourages others to realize their full potential.

The 2023 college football season was filled with controversy as Deion "Primetime" Sanders took his position as head coach of the Colorado Buffaloes. Prior to the start of the season, there was speculation about his style of leadership, and whether he would be good enough to lead the team to victory. The previous team and coach had a record of 1-11 and ranked 128 out of 131 teams. To say the team was bad was an understatement. They needed a total overhaul and that's what Coach Primetime offered. This would not be his first college coaching position, but it was his first Division I position. The new season kicked off with many celebrity appearances including Dwayne "the Rock" Johnson to Lil' Wayne, offering fanfare and celebrity-ship, and many wondered if that would be enough to win games. Rival coaches, sportscasters, and podcasters chimed in doubting his ability to lead his team to victory.

The first game was a surprising victory, beating their opponent by 3 points. They were off to a great start and started to muzzle the hateful remarks of the doubters. However, by a few games in, things began to unravel and the hyped enthusiasm resulted in back-to-back losses. As the team started to lose games week after week, there was an unspoken alliance formed by Sanders' supporters. They began to highlight his leadership and how he changed the face of college football. They started acknowledging that his off-the-field record was much better than his on-the- field record. The young men he coached talked about his fatherhood approach, his life lessons taught in football practices, and how he genuinely loved the players not for their talents, but who they were as individuals. The commentators couldn't deny the impact he had as his leadership became the focus of the conversation. In the end, the true win had been the lives he had impacted and the millions of viewers that tuned in each week, many of whom were not college football fans. Coach Prime ended the season with a 4-8 record. Not exactly the Return of the Titans comeback many had hoped for, but it was indeed an improvement from where the team started, with a new coaching staff and new players. The story doesn't end there, his flashy and bold style of leadership resulted in Colorado football games generating an estimated $113.2 million for the Boulder economy.

> **“Great leadership fosters a culture of collaboration, innovation, and continuous improvement. Ultimately, this extends far beyond the workplace, shaping the lives of those who are fortunate enough to be led by truly exceptional individuals.”**

In the realm of leadership, certain attributes set apart the good from the great. These characteristics are not just inherent traits but skills honed through experience, reflection, and a conscious effort to adapt and inspire. The attributes of great leaders include a fluid personality, adaptability, the ability to create an inclusive environment, and being culture shifters. These are not all innate qualities but can be developed over time. These traits are interdependent, each amplifying the effect of the others. Leaders who cultivate these attributes not only achieve personal and organizational success but also leave a lasting impact, inspiring the next generation to carry the torch forward.

Fluid Personality: The Chameleon Trait

A fluid personality does not imply inconsistency or lack of principles. Instead, it represents a leader's ability to navigate through diverse situations and groups with ease and grace. Leaders possessing a fluid personality are like chameleons, adept at adjusting their approach based on the audience and the context, ensuring their message is not just heard but felt and understood. This ability to morph without losing one's core identity is fundamental in today's globalized and multicultural work environments. It allows leaders to connect deeply with individuals from various backgrounds, fostering a sense of unity and shared purpose.

Adaptability: The Art of Graceful Evolution

In a world where change is the only constant, adaptability stands out as a non-negotiable attribute for great leaders. It's about having the foresight to anticipate changes and the agility to pivot strategies and plans without losing momentum. Adaptability goes hand in hand with resilience—the capacity to face setbacks and challenges without being defeated. Leaders who embody adaptability do not merely react to change; they proactively prepare for it, leading their teams through uncharted territories with confidence and poise. This trait ensures that organizations not only survive but also thrive amidst uncertainty.

Inclusivity Champions

Great leaders create inclusive environments. Leadership is as much about nurturing others as it is about achieving goals. Great leaders understand the power of making everyone feel heard and respected. This involves actively listening, valuing diverse perspectives, and creating a culture where feedback is not just encouraged but celebrated. By doing so, leaders unlock the full potential of their teams, fostering innovation and a sense of ownership. An inclusive environment is one where every team member feels they belong, regardless of their background, role, or level of experience. In such environments, people are more engaged, committed, and motivated to contribute their best.

Culture Shifters

Great leaders are culture shifters and pioneers of change. They possess the vision to see beyond the status quo and the courage to challenge it. Culture shifters understand that to enact real change, one must address the underlying beliefs, values, and behaviors that define an organization. They lead by example, embodying the values they wish to see while inspiring others to follow suit. By fostering a culture of innovation, integrity, and inclusivity, they pave the way for sustainable growth and success.

Great Leaders Build Great Teams

To build an effective team, leaders must recognize their individual strengths and weaknesses. It's common for business owners to gravitate towards people who mirror their strengths, thinking it creates harmony. However, this approach can lead to problems. If you are not aware of your weaknesses, you will fall into the trap of hiring individuals whom you feel you can relate to, assuming it will lead to better understanding and collaboration. On the contrary, this mindset can be detrimental. While team members need to align on core values such as honesty and directness, diversity in communication styles and personalities is equally vital. Personal experience has taught me that replicating one's own traits in team members can backfire. Having self-awareness will enable you to identify the areas of your business that require you to hire and then delegate those tasks to team members. You want to build your team in the areas where you are weak. By doing so, you can focus on the work that you enjoy and excel at, while your team supports you in other areas.

For example, if you are weak in accounting, find someone who excels in this area to support you. I don't like accounting, although I earned an A in the class and graduated with an MBA. I excel in marketing and have strong communication skills, which allows me to effectively convey my company's vision and attract the right people. I have accountants and attorneys on my team who specialize in the areas I don't or have the time to learn. By leveraging their expertise, I can keep my business compliant while earning enough revenue to pay for their services. My accounting and legal firms are among the best in Florida and are the same ones that a big company like Tesla would use. I recognize that I cannot be good at everything, so I focus on my strengths and build my team around them. This has allowed me to create multiple successful businesses.

Building wealth is an incredible personal development journey. It's crucial to have team members who share your core values rather than identical personalities. Diversity in personalities is key for a successful team. You wouldn't want everyone to be a carbon copy of yourself. When you do the work and build your leadership capacity, you will attract like-minded people. These individuals will share your values and work ethic, making your brand stronger.

Your Role as Leader

As the leader, you should have a clear vision and goals established before bringing anyone new into your company. As you lead and grow your business, as the CEO and visionary, define what you expect from every individual in your organization. Inform them of your core values. Make sure they understand the mission statement and are in alignment with your vision. Communicating these aspects effectively during the onboarding process is key to ensuring that new hires are in sync with your company's direction and goals. Starting off on the right foot is vital, as it sets the tone for the employee's journey within your organization and can significantly impact retention rates and overall business success. Investing time, effort, and resources into proper training, onboarding, and alignment with your company's culture are ways to cultivate the desired organizational environment. As mentioned earlier, as a CEO, you have an important role as the visionary and decision-maker of your company. To ensure the success of your vision, you need a team that supports and implements it. To achieve this, you need to become a leader that people will follow. Successful businesses stand out not only for their financial achievements but also for their commitment to cultivating a positive and inclusive work culture. Recognizing the importance of workplace culture is paramount, as it shapes employee contentment, efficiency, and ultimately, the growth of your business.

I deeply value the strong bonds I share with my team. We support and protect each other like family. There have been instances where I've had to use my personal credit card to pay my employees, a testament to the unity and loyalty we have. My experiences at other firms with great cultures, like Movement Mortgage and South Star Funding, exposed me to company-paid outings to locations like St. Thomas, Virgin Islands, which resulted in lifelong memories and even personal relationships. These experiences served as inspiration for the culture of support and togetherness the organization fostered.

Build a Supportive Environment

One of the best things you can do for yourself on your journey to wealth is to create a success-supportive environment. This is an environment(s) that supports your growth and celebrates you for the amazing person you are. It should be an environment that you feel comfortable in, one that you don't need to wear a mask or try to prove who you are. You can be free to be you! This kind of environment is designed to uplift you, encourage your personal growth, and acknowledge your worth. It should be a space where you feel safe, respected, and valued for being your authentic self without the need to conform or prove anything to others. Surrounding yourself with positivity, inspiration, and support can significantly impact your mindset and motivation towards reaching your goals. In this nurturing environment, you should feel empowered to pursue your dreams, take risks, and embrace your uniqueness without fear of judgment.

Cultivating such a space can include surrounding yourself with like-minded individuals who share your ambitions, engaging in activities that inspire and challenge you, and creating a physical space that reflects your aspirations and values. By fostering a success-supportive environment, you are setting yourself up for success by harnessing the power of positivity and encouragement in your journey towards wealth and fulfillment. Everything is about energy—the kind you give and the kind you receive. Similarly, the energy we absorb from our environment and the people we surround ourselves with can shape our own mindsets and emotions. By being mindful of the energy we give and receive, we can cultivate a more harmonious and fulfilling life for ourselves and those around us.

The Planner, The Implementer, The Innovator, The Seller

In the bustling world of entrepreneurship, building a successful business is akin to assembling a championship-winning sports team. Each member plays a crucial role, contributing their unique skills and perspectives towards a common goal. For entrepreneurs embarking on this journey, understanding the types of people essential to their team is paramount. These include The Planner, The Implementer, The Innovator, and The Seller. Each of these roles brings a distinct set of skills and attributes that, when combined, can propel a business to new heights.

The Planner is the strategist of the group. They are adept at setting goals, identifying the steps needed to achieve them, and foreseeing potential obstacles. Their ability to think ahead and plan meticulously ensures that the business remains focused and on track. The Planner is indispensable in transforming vision into actionable strategies, making them a foundational pillar of any successful team.

The Implementer is the one who gets things done. They take the plans and strategies developed by the Planner and turn them into reality. With a keen eye for detail and a hands-on approach, the Implementer oversees the day-to-day operations, ensuring that each task is executed efficiently and effectively. They are problem solvers, often finding creative solutions to unexpected challenges. Their relentless drive and ability to translate plans into action make them the engine of the team, driving the business forward.

The Innovator is the creative powerhouse, always thinking outside the box. They bring a fresh perspective to the team; challenging conventional wisdom and introducing new ideas. The Innovator thrives on change and experimentation, constantly seeking ways to improve products, services, or processes. Their creativity not only sparks innovation within the team but also helps the business adapt and evolve in a fast-changing market.

The Seller is the charismatic communicator, adept at persuading and influencing others. They are the face of the business, connecting with customers, partners, and investors. The Seller has a deep understanding of the market and the needs of the customers, enabling them to effectively market and sell the business's products or services. Their ability to build relationships and generate revenue is critical to the survival and growth of the business.

Who you bring along with you on the journey to wealth is important. Every workplace or brand should have a workplace culture. If you don't have one just yet, take some time to plan this out before you build your team. If you don't, you will find yourself attracting employees who work against you instead of with you. I have had my share of not-so-good employees. People who were excited to meet Noelle "the brand and influencer" but could not respect or honor the work ethic that was needed to help the brand continue to grow and thrive. You want to build your team with people that understand your brand culture. "A brand culture is the system of beliefs, values, experiences, and material traits of a company, shared between employees and society. Brand culture is about connecting the image you present to the outside world with the values inside the company."[14]

PICK A HORSE

I am dedicated to fostering a culture centered around delivering value, a principle I consistently emphasize to my team within my company. Our primary focus is ensuring that students achieve their desired outcomes by equipping them with the necessary tools and resources while providing unwavering support aligned with their vision. We have a structured plan in place to execute on these objectives and maintain optimistic attitudes, embodying our values in our actions. This commitment to value creation is ingrained in our everyday interactions with anyone associated with the company, whether they are customers, clients, students, or colleagues. Cultivating this culture is a continuous effort, akin to nurturing the values within a family over the years.

Now, 10 years later, my team continues to help me grow and transform the brand. My brand, which originally focused on real estate investing, has expanded into education, coaching, books, property management, and more. As you build, you need members on your team who can expand and help you seamlessly launch new products and services. You also need team members who can serve clients with the utmost level of support. You need team members who think outside the box, those who offer solutions instead of problems, and those who aspire to be part of something amazing.

The Changing Work Environment

The traditional workplace landscape has evolved significantly, and the concept of the workplace has shifted to the employees' homes. To ensure continuous connectivity, various technologies like Slack and Google Chat are utilized for communication. Building and sustaining meaningful relationships with customers, clients, contractors, and industry peers is paramount. Establishing communication routines, such as daily check-ins with team members and weekly departmental meetings, form the foundation for fostering these crucial connections. My support team (mainly my employees and contractors) has transitioned to working remotely; the office space for my real estate brokerage remains largely vacant. As real estate professionals, our work is predominantly conducted on the go, utilizing mobile devices. As a result, my managers regularly engage with their teams, even if for a brief period each morning, to maintain rapport. While physical office presence is no longer a necessity, fostering team unity remains a focus. To nurture this, we host an annual team gathering in Florida. During this event, team members stay together in a rented Airbnb, engaging in team-building activities to strengthen connections.

Instill Your Company's Values

Companies that prioritize instilling their values and mission in every employee from the very beginning, during orientation and onboarding, tend to foster a sense of purpose and unity among their workforce. Clear communication about the company's history, vision, and goals is important in aligning employees with the company's objectives and creating a shared sense of direction. This focus on building a cohesive and motivated team will allow you to run a successful business, regardless of its size. In my experience, businesses that invest in their employees' understanding of the company's purpose and values often see higher levels of engagement, loyalty, and overall success.

Attract the Right Team Players and Put Them in the Right Positions

Top Level Positions

As you build your success team, you want to think about the areas in your business that are required for the sustainability of the company. I want to address the top three positions that are critical and require your best players: **Sales, Marketing, and Customer Service.**

Sales

In the early stages of a business, the CEO often takes on the role of the lead salesperson. As a new entrepreneur, while it's important to focus on building a strong team, the reality for most is that they don't have the luxury of starting with a large amount of venture capital. Instead, many start by bootstrapping their businesses using their own funds, business credit, and personal savings. This means that generating sales from the outset is crucial to keeping the business afloat, even if other operational aspects may not be going as smoothly. Therefore, the first priority when forming a team for a new company should often be focused on sales, as this is what sustains the business in the early stages, while other details can be ironed out along the way.

Sales are the lifeline of any team within a company, playing a pivotal role in its success. This doesn't mean other areas of the business, like customer service, fulfillment, accounting, and other functions are not essential; however, sales stand out as the driving force behind revenue generation. While marketing focuses on promoting and advertising the business to attract leads, the sales department is responsible for converting those leads into customers. A strong focus on sales, including pricing strategies and articulating the value proposition, is essential for securing new customers.

Marketing

One aspect of companies that keep luxury brands, such as Chanel, profitable is their strategic approach to product releases and ensuring exclusivity and maintaining their high value. The meticulous thought and creativity behind Chanel's clothing, accessories, and jewelry collections are evident in their timeless elegance, despite any controversies surrounding the brand. The lasting value and innovation displayed by Chanel's products, exemplify the power of strategic marketing and design in creating a lasting legacy in the fashion industry.

When examining the areas of marketing and sales systems in large corporations, it is evident that mastering marketing strategies is paramount. Effective marketing tactics, such as promoting the brand, products, and services are needed for attracting and retaining customers. Marketing is imperative to attract people to your business. Once the leads are generated, the sales team steps in to convert these potential customers into actual clients.

WHO'S COMING WITH YOU?

It's not uncommon for me to coach individuals who dive right into establishing a routine centered on marketing and sales, sometimes even before having physical inventory. They kick off with just a website, showcasing the products and services. Once they start generating income, they use the revenue to purchase inventory for customers. The modern business landscape offers a wealth of opportunities to jumpstart marketing and sales efforts, allowing you to grow your customer base, and enhance customer service. If you still have your 9-5 job, it can be difficult to balance your time between your job and your business. However, it is important to make marketing a priority and to consistently dedicate time to it. This can be done by setting aside specific hours each week to focus solely on marketing efforts. Additionally, it is important to follow up with leads that did not convert in order to continue building relationships and potentially convert them in the future.

Overall, consistency is key when it comes to entrepreneurship. By consistently marketing your business, you can generate a steady stream of leads and customers, which can lead to long-term growth. It is important to always be marketing your business, even if you have a steady stream of income from a full-time job. In order to grow your business, you must reinvest your profits into marketing efforts such as paying for ads and any other method you choose to get the word out. This will help you consistently generate leads and convert them into customers.

Customer Service

Developing a good customer service team is critical for any organization since it directly affects client satisfaction, loyalty, and overall success. With the support of a competent customer service team, problems can be resolved quickly, relationships with customers can be strengthened, and the brand's reputation can be elevated. Businesses that provide exceptional service set themselves apart from competitors, enhance client retention, and attract new customers through positive word-of-mouth.

There are several approaches for determining the effectiveness of a customer service team. One frequent method is to conduct customer feedback questionnaires or ratings after encounters with the team. To gauge the team's efficiency, it's helpful to keep an eye on KPIs like response and resolution times, customer satisfaction ratings, and renewal rates. Regular training sessions, role-playing scenarios, and performance reviews can all help to improve the team's performance and ensure that they fulfill the established criteria of excellence.

The key to maintaining strong relationships with customers, clients, and partners, lies in establishing routines and automating tasks within those routines. By scheduling calls and meetings and ensuring they are visible to all parties involved, you create a sense of organization and reliability. Consistent communication through phone calls, emails, and reminders, as well as automating some of these interactions, plays a crucial role in nurturing these relationships. It's essential to keep channels of communication open and reach out regularly, even if the other party hasn't initiated contact recently. By setting up automated messages to check in periodically, you can stay connected without the need to remember every detail.

Additional Supporting Team Members:

Outside of the three roles previously discussed, you should also consider hiring or contracting other members for your team as your budget allows, including:

Accounting

This role is essential for managing finances, tracking expenses, and ensuring compliance with tax laws. It helps business owners make informed decisions based on financial data and maintain financial stability.

Legal

The legal team is vital to protect the business from risks and ensure compliance with laws and regulations. A solid legal framework can safeguard intellectual property, contracts, and overall business operations.

Operations Manager

Operations managers are responsible for overseeing day-to-day activities, optimizing processes, and ensuring smooth workflow. Their role is crucial in maintaining efficiency, quality control, and meeting business objectives.

Virtual Assistants

The virtual assistant handles various administrative tasks, freeing up time for you to focus on core activities and strategic planning. They can handle tasks such as emails, document preparation, research, and support other departments.

Events Team

The events team plays a significant role in marketing, branding, and customer engagement. They play a crucial role in overseeing the planning, coordination, and execution of events aimed at promoting the business, building relationships, and attracting new clients. Their responsibilities also include developing event strategies, managing budgets, coordinating logistics, and ensuring seamless event delivery.

Social Media

A social media manager plays a key role in shaping the digital image and communication of the organization in the online world. They are responsible for creating and curating engaging content for various social media platforms.

Product/ Services Development

Professionals in this role are responsible for researching market trends, understanding customer needs, and collaborating with various departments to create innovative products or services. They play a key role from conceptualization to launch. They should be creative, analytical, and strategic thinkers to successfully introduce new products/services that resonate with customers and drive business growth.

Media and Technology

This team plays a vital role in shaping your business's online presence. They manage and create content for various digital platforms such as websites and email campaigns to ensure you reach your target audience. They also monitor and analyze data and metrics to optimize strategies and improve performance, staying up-to-date with the latest trends and technologies in the digital space.

Your Home Team

I believe that building your behind-the-scenes home team is just as important as building your out-front business team. I don't think we put enough emphasis on the impact that a supportive spouse and children can have on our business results. As you are building your business, factor in your family. Have conversations and set expectations before problems arise. Set them on your calendar and check in with them to ensure they don't feel neglected or left out. There are times when your business will require more of your attention. Don't just assume your family should understand. They should be a part of your growth plan as well. These are the people who will remain consistent with you whether you make a million dollars or not. Factor in time and consideration for your home team.

Who's <u>Not</u> Coming With You?

A group of people were sitting in a boat. One person pulled out a hand drill and proceeded to drill a hole beneath their seat.

The fellow passengers screamed at the incredulous sight and asked, "What do you think you're doing?!"

The hole driller dismissed the question and responded, "What do you care? Am I not drilling under my seat?"

They replied: "Because you are sinking the boat with us in it!"[15]

- Rabbi Shimon bar Yochai

Not too far off from survivor's remorse is the idea that everyone can come on this journey with you. Go ahead and make peace with the idea that your winner's circle would most likely be different from those that are to the right and left of you today. Just as you need to identify who's coming with you—you also need to identify who isn't. This is a good time to remove any person out of your life that does not help you elevate or grow to this next level. This may mean cutting loose the close family and friends, relationships, or organizations that keep you distracted. Yes, even that person (the one that just crossed your mind). This may mean firing any team member that doesn't add value to the organization and disrespects the culture you are building.

Take some time and reflect on this. Everyone can't cross this threshold with you. This move will be the one that helps you safely arrive to the other side without any holes in your boat. As Gandhi said, we must embody the change we wish to see, serving as the guiding light and role model within our organization.

Leadership Assessment Questionnaire for Entrepreneurs

As you embark on your entrepreneurial journey, understanding your leadership style, strengths, and areas for improvement is essential. This assessment is designed to help you reflect on your leadership capabilities and envision the culture you wish to cultivate in your business. Your responses will not only provide insights into your current leadership capabilities but also guide you in setting intentional goals for personal and professional growth as an entrepreneur. Remember, leadership is a journey, not a destination, and embracing continuous learning and self-reflection is key to becoming an effective leader.

Take your time to answer these questions honestly and thoughtfully.

1. **Areas of Strength:**

    o What do you consider your top three leadership strengths?

    o Can you provide examples of how you have effectively used these strengths in a professional setting?

2. **Areas of Weakness:**

    o Identify up to three areas where you feel your leadership skills could be improved.

    o Reflecting on past experiences, can you recall any situations where these weaknesses impacted your team or project outcomes?

3. **Strategies for Improvement:**

    o For each area of weakness identified, what specific actions can you take to develop these skills?

    o Are there any resources (e.g., books, courses, mentors) you plan to utilize to aid in your development?

4. **Vision for Workplace Culture:**

    o Describe the workplace culture you aim to establish in your business. Consider aspects such as communication style, team collaboration, decision-making processes, and work-life balance.

WHO'S COMING WITH YOU?

- How do your leadership strengths support the creation of this culture? Conversely, how might your weaknesses pose challenges, and how do you plan to address them?

5. **Leadership Role Models:**

    - Who are your leadership role models, and what aspects of their leadership style do you aspire to emulate in your entrepreneurial journey?

    - How will incorporating these elements into your leadership approach help you in building the desired workplace culture?

6. **Feedback and Continuous Learning:**

    - How do you plan to seek and incorporate feedback from your team about your leadership style and the workplace culture?

    - Describe your approach to fostering a culture of continuous learning and improvement for yourself and your team.

7. **Adapting to Change:**

    o   Entrepreneurship often involves navigating uncertainty and change. How do you plan to adapt your leadership style in response to changing circumstances within your business or industry?

    o   What strategies will you employ to ensure your team remains resilient and motivated during times of change?

Chapter Review

○ Vision, honesty, and empathy are among the traits of a leader that can inspire people to strive for a common objective.

○ Great leadership fosters a culture of collaboration, innovation, and continuous improvement.

○ While it's important for team members to align on core values such as honesty and directness, diversity in communication styles and personalities is equally vital.

○ Investing time, effort, and resources into proper training, onboarding, and alignment with your company's culture are ways to cultivate the desired organizational environment.

○ Companies that prioritize instilling their values and mission in every employee from the very beginning, during orientation and onboarding, tend to foster a sense of purpose and unity among their workforce.

CHAPTER EIGHT
What's Your Story?

WHILE FILING MY annual taxes in 2015, my accountant casually mentioned that my real estate portfolio was valued at a million dollars in equity. I didn't have a million dollars in the bank; however, my properties were worth a million—on paper I was a millionaire. *I was a millionaire and didn't know it?!* In case you're wondering if I started celebrating by buying cars, taking exotic trips, and living the champagne life, the answer is, no. My response was pretty boring. There was no dancing on my accountant's desk, colorful confetti drops, or dramatic fanfare. The truth is, I didn't feel any different. In my mind, I had become a millionaire long before it was manifested while I was working my corporate job earning a fraction of what a millionaire earns.

WHAT'S YOUR STORY?

I often teach there are three ways to become a millionaire.

> #1) Acquiring a portfolio valued at $1,000,000 (In my case—real estate)
>
> #2) Having $1,000,000 in liquid cash
>
> #3) $1,000,000 annual salary (You earn $83,333 per month)

When I decided I wanted to become a millionaire, I began incorporating millionaire affirmations into my daily routine. Becoming a millionaire first starts in your mind. The thoughts then translate into your actions. What you believe before you see it manifest will determine how you handle your money, your affairs, and your boundaries. In other words—if you say you want to become financially wealthy, what do your actions say? Are they in alignment with this? Have you shifted your actions to include what wealthy people do? The way this works is to manifest it in your mind and actions before you can manifest it in your physical life. Hearing my accountant tell me I was a millionaire was just a confirmation of what I already knew about myself. I knew that if I kept doing the work, showing up every day, and being consistent with my purpose, I would arrive at the right time. I had a daily

PICK A HORSE

routine of closing my eyes and seeing myself making millions and living a life of freedom. My vision never faltered. During that time, I was profiting somewhere around $60,000 by wholesaling properties while working part-time in real estate. I made a decision and started on a path of doing the inner work to attract wealth.

Secrets of the Millionaire Mind: Mastering the Inner Game of Wealth by T. Harv Eker is a book that offers valuable insights into the mindset and habits of successful individuals who have achieved financial abundance. One key takeaway from the book is the importance of developing a positive money mindset. Eker emphasizes the power of thoughts and beliefs in shaping one's financial reality, highlighting the significance of adopting a mindset of abundance rather than scarcity.

After that meeting in my CPA's office, I began working diligently on ways to increase my sales. I attended more workshops, hired additional coaches, and learned more about adding additional streams of income within my scope of coaching. I became more active in my social media presence as well. I didn't have a large staff at the time—it was me and my virtual assistant putting together e-mail campaigns, following up on leads, creating products, and closing deals. I also launched my live real estate tours. This was a power move for me.

WHAT'S YOUR STORY?

During those events, I would drive groups of 10-15 event attendees in a van and show them my various fix-and-flip projects, as well as my properties on my real estate portfolio. I taught them the process of acquiring properties and showed them how they could become wealthy doing real estate.

As an added value, I sold my coaching services and formed partnerships with my students. It was a win-win for everyone. This strategy allowed me to save thousands of dollars on business marketing. They would locate the real estate deals, based on the criteria I taught them, and I would either pay a referral fee or provide the financing if it was a good fit. The leads were brought directly to me, some with hundreds of thousands of dollars in equity.

That was a major time of my personal growth. I started to understand the value of my gift and I was able to get rid of the imposter syndrome. I became confident in what I offered to the world. Throughout that year, my funds rapidly increased. In 2019, when I sat in front of the CPA ready to file my taxes, he revealed that I had hit the million-dollar mark, not only in my real estate portfolio but also in liquid cash! It felt good to have worked so hard to achieve that milestone. This is what it will take for you to achieve your goals as well. There isn't a magical formula. I made a decision about what I wanted, and then every day, I affirmed it. I would say I was a millionaire and believed that everything was always working in my favor. I would repeat affirmations to myself, "I attract wealth effortlessly, and others are eager to engage in commerce and transactions with me." I then put in the work by creating strategies for partnerships and growth that were in alignment.

Don't Be Ashamed of Your Story

There was another component I believe that set me apart, and that was my relatability. People could see themselves in my story of losing everything in the pursuit of financial freedom. Coach Lisa taught me the power of storytelling and how we can connect with people, as customers do business with people they like and trust. But even further than that, they do business with people who have "receipts." Everything I have shared so far is the successful actions and principles that have generated millions of dollars. Despite my academic and professional background, I am still human and want to connect with you by sharing my vulnerabilities. My company, Noelle Randall Coaching, specializes in assisting individuals who are making the transition from employee to real estate entrepreneur. Our ultimate goal is to teach others how to leverage real estate investments to become millionaires. This is the purpose of our YouTube channel, TikTok, and other media platforms. That is the purpose of this book. By sharing my personal stories, I hope to show you that it is achievable.

As a successful CEO, I understand the value of sharing my personal story. I often tell my story of losing everything, filing for bankruptcy, and living in my parent's basement to becoming financially independent. This vulnerability helps me to connect with people on a deeper level. When they hear my story, they know I understand their struggle and it helps me to establish trust and credibility. This approach has not only helped me secure real estate deals but also made me a relatable and effective leader. As a CEO, it's essential to know how to tell your story and understand how it aligns with your company's values and mission. This is what we teach at my company. That is the purpose of my YouTube channel. That is the purpose of my TikTok. That is the purpose of my social media. That is the purpose of this book. This is my mission.

I love sharing my wins with my followers. With each new accomplishment, I make sure to share it with them and I show them how I did it. I don't want to become another bragging coach; I want to be a source of inspiration and motivation. I want others to know that they can do great

PICK A HORSE

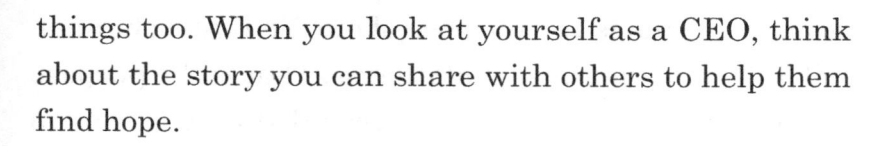

things too. When you look at yourself as a CEO, think about the story you can share with others to help them find hope.

What obstacles have you overcome?

What are your vulnerabilities?

What are you especially good at?

What gives you credibility?

What distinguishes you as someone that others should emulate and follow?

What is your backstory?

WHAT'S YOUR STORY?

When you create your story in a way that resonates with others, you will see how much easier it is to build your brand. People are looking for authenticity to connect with. They are waiting to hear your story of overcoming. I want to encourage you to overcome any fears or reservations you have about connecting with others. Telling your story with authenticity involves being true to yourself and sharing your experiences in a genuine and sincere manner. To do this effectively, it's important to reflect on your own thoughts, feelings, and beliefs, and express them honestly. Authentic storytelling also involves being vulnerable and open about your struggles, successes, and emotions as this can create a deeper connection with your audience.

One way to tell your story authentically is to focus on the details that make it unique to you. Share personal anecdotes, memories, and insights that others may not have experienced. Additionally, being mindful of your audience and tailoring your message to resonate with them, can help create a more authentic connection. Ultimately, authenticity in storytelling comes from being true to yourself, sharing your experiences sincerely, and connecting with others on a human level. By embracing your individuality and speaking from the heart, you can effectively communicate your story in a way that is genuine and compelling.

Chapter Review

○ People do business with people who have "receipts."

○ As a CEO, it's essential to know how to tell your story and understand how it aligns with your company's values and mission.

○ Telling your story with authenticity involves being true to yourself and sharing your experiences in a genuine and sincere manner. To do this effectively, it's important to reflect on your own thoughts, feelings, and beliefs, and express them honestly.

Let's Talk

SCAN HERE

Call Noelle

CallNoelle.com

CHAPTER NINE

What If You Fail?

In 2015, I began dipping my toe in the professional speaker circuit. After some strategy calls with my coach, I launched into the deep. I was profitable in my real estate business by then and was becoming more comfortable in the real estate coaching arena. It was time for me to host a live event in Houston, Texas. It wasn't my first event; however, it was a newer, bigger market. The housing market had steady growth in Houston, making it an ideal location for real estate investors and potential connections. The event marked a significant transition from my events in Dallas and opened a new market and wealth of connections. *Count me in!*

My team and I outlined the event objectives, identified an ideal venue, and organized the marketing strategy. To sprinkle a bit of glitz, I added a celebrity face as a

WHAT IF YOU FAIL?

highlight of the evening. We planned and executed flawlessly to ensure there would be a great turnout. The marketing strategy entailed reaching out to my extensive email list, running local ads and connecting with local Houstonians that I knew and asking them for their support by inviting their friends. I felt good about how hard we'd worked. After months of preparation, the day of the event finally arrived. My husband drove me from Dallas to Houston Texas; an easy four-hour trip. We checked into the Hilton and my team stepped into full gear to prepare and set up the room. The chairs were set up, table covers were placed on the tables, and my books were displayed in each guest chair—everything was on schedule. After the conference room was fully prepared, I went up to my room to dress and prepare for my presentation. I left my team in place to greet the guests and to put out any last-minute fires.

The registration list included over 100 people and the room was set up accordingly. Although the event was free, the plan was to sell my real estate coaching program offer from the stage. The $15,000 investment that I paid to host the event, was a drop in the bucket compared to the sales I would make that night. The meeting was scheduled somewhere between 4-5 pm (I later discovered that's not a good time to start). However, with over 100 registrants, if at least 50 showed up on time we would

PICK A HORSE

be fine. When it came time for the event to begin, there were just a few people there, so I gave a bit more time for them to arrive as Houston's traffic can be a nightmare. By 6 pm, my mentor and guest motioned for me to start.

Six people eagerly awaited my presentation.
Six out of 100+ registrants
Six was the final count....

I gave myself a pep talk, walked out and delivered my PowerPoint presentation as if the room was filled. At the end of the presentation, there were two enrollees into my program. *Not too bad when you consider the conversion rates.* To express how deeply disheartened I felt can't really be put into words, but the blow of cashing out $15,000 on a hotel venue, professional photographer, celebrity guest appearance, my entire team, and travel accommodations was gut-wrenching. The next morning, I couldn't move. The pillow was soaked with tears and I barely had any energy. I am so thankful my husband was there to hold me. He and my assistant made sure I ate breakfast before we headed back to Dallas. I was overwhelmed with emotions. Nevertheless, I didn't quit.

After some time, I got back on the horse, evaluated what worked and where I had made mistakes, and adjusted my future events and marketing accordingly. I concluded

WHAT IF YOU FAIL?

that free events are often less attended as people don't value things they don't have to pay for. Despite the temporary setback, I acknowledged the disappointment, reframed it as a learning opportunity, and gathered the strength to persevere.

Facing rejection is a common experience for many successful individuals, especially those who aspire to become wealthy CEOs of organizations. Rejection, whether in the form of business proposals, or personal endeavors, can be disheartening and challenging. The ability to handle rejection is a crucial attribute for a CEO, as it demonstrates resilience, determination, and perseverance. Like the CEO of Canva, Melanie, if you are rejected over 100 times, will you continue on your path towards your goals? How disappointing she must have felt after hearing so many no's on a product she believed in and knew would work. Maybe she knew Canva would be worth billions one day, but I highly doubt she did. When you are faced with rejections and defeats, you can't let that stop you. The saying goes, "Every no you receive puts you one step closer to your yes."[16]

The questions you must answer are, *Will you have the patience and perseverance to keep showing up? Will you maintain your enthusiasm and motivation when nothing seems to go as planned? Will you continue to host live*

PICK A HORSE

events even if people don't show up to support you? Can you look rejection in the face and take your power back? This is what it will take to be financially free. Being financially free requires a strong mindset to navigate through rejection, criticism, and adversities. It's about turning rejection into motivation, using it as a stepping stone towards growth and success. I have shared personal aspects of my journey. I am not ashamed to admit that I failed at least a dozen times in multiple businesses before I achieved success.

You might wonder why you should listen to me or read my book after so many setbacks. The truth is, failure is not the end. There is no such thing as failure. It's important to understand that many times what we perceive as failure is simply giving up when faced with challenges or uncertainty. In other words, we quit right before we experience the breakthrough we want. Yes, encountering obstacles in business or dealing with returns and cancellations can be disheartening. However, it's crucial to embrace these setbacks as learning experiences rather than failures. You can't let the loss of a big contract or what you consider to be a large client discourage you and cause you to quit. Whether they stay or leave—guess what? You're going to be just fine. By persisting through difficulties, we pave the way for growth and eventual success.

WHAT IF YOU FAIL?

It wasn't until I was nearly 30 that I finally earned my college degree while living in my parents' basement. Yet by the time I turned 36, I had become a millionaire. This transformation in my life serves as a reminder that setbacks and failures are often integral parts of the journey to success. Success doesn't come without its share of setbacks; it's all about learning through trial and error. Just like a compass that needs movement to point you in the right direction, in life, you have to start taking action to pave your path forward. Just as our GPS systems can't guide us until we begin moving, in life, progress requires us to take the first step toward our goals.

I am extremely passionate about business and the value of developing a strong wealth growth plan and then sticking to it. While challenges or delays are common, the goal is to never quit until you reach your success threshold. If the first plan didn't work out, take time to evaluate the plan, make any required revisions, and keep moving forward. Many people fail to attain their goals because they give up too quickly at the first indication of adversity. Rather than instantly switching to a new strategy or abandoning current efforts, it is critical to remain engaged and adaptable. Remember, just because things aren't going as planned, doesn't mean success is impossible. At times, it may be necessary to take a different route to reach your destination but don't

PICK A HORSE

change the destination. Roadblocks, such as construction on the highway, or street detours, do not mean you need to abort traveling altogether. Roadblocks shouldn't indicate a standstill in your progress. It may put you at a temporary delay but it shouldn't cancel your trip.

How will you handle adversity in business? Let's say for instance, that your goal was to secure 12 clients this month. However, during your end-of-the-month audit, you notice that you have only acquired five. To make matters worse, three of the five cancel, leaving you with just two. Can this be disappointing? Of course! it can. But this setback does not mean your plan is doomed to fail. Rather than scrapping the plan or assuming you're doing something drastically wrong, view these challenges as learning opportunities. Reflect on why your numbers were low. Perhaps more follow-ups were needed or more calls should have been made? Reflect on why the clients canceled – was something lacking in the service? Were they your ideal client or did you book them out of desperation to hit your sales target? The key is not to doubt the plan itself but to evaluate your execution of it. Remember, any well-thought-out plan has the potential to succeed if you diligently put it into action.

After what many would consider a failed event, I used it as an opportunity to practice my presentation skills.

WHAT IF YOU FAIL?

I delivered my talk as if there were hundreds of people staring back at me. I didn't allow that one moment to stop me. If I would had allowed disappointment to silence my voice, you wouldn't be reading this right now. I wouldn't have had the opportunity to coach so many amazing people and receive the testimonials that I get to read almost daily.

I frequently share my experiences to help aspiring entrepreneurs understand what it takes. Things will not always go exactly as you anticipate. When I find myself at this juncture, I allow myself to have an emotional dump. I process the emotions. I allow myself to fully express my emotions. I allow myself to express sadness and to grieve, just as one would when dealing with a loss. It's critical to understand that setbacks are normal, and it's okay to be frustrated when things don't go as planned. Although I may feel down temporarily, I bounce back quickly because that is not the end of my story.

By using mantras and conducting inner work, I remind myself that everything is going as it should and that problems are opportunities for growth. This perspective keeps me motivated and hopeful, knowing that better days are coming and that I am constantly growing.

> **❝ Great leaders know that development is a necessity - not a "nice to have." They're obsessed with personal growth and relentlessly focused on growing their leadership qualities."**[17]

Personal development is key to surviving and thriving, especially when going through tough situations. Like exercise, this technique takes consistent effort and time spent practicing. Just as strength training with heavier weights increases physical strength, mental toughness training with regular practice increases resilience. Building mental strength requires perseverance and growth, similar to progressively lifting heavier weights or running longer distances. You can change your thinking and do great things in life, work, or business if you constantly push yourself and tell yourself positive things.

The way you communicate with yourself plays a significant role in how you tackle challenges and build mental resilience. During tough times, when negative thoughts cloud your mind, it's crucial to shift your focus by engaging in positive self-talk. To drown out internal and external distractions and maintain your concentration on your objectives, consider minimizing exposure to negative or toxic external stimuli. By silencing these external influences, you create space to reinforce positive internal messages and affirmations. Instead of criticizing yourself, replace those thoughts with empowering statements to uplift your spirit and bolster your confidence. If you want to strengthen your mind, you must avoid things that drain your energy, such as comparison, gossip, and bad news. Recognizing the distractions that inhibit your success is essential for strengthening your mental resilience. Negative emotions and self-doubt can result from behaviors like watching too much television, surfing through social media, or constantly comparing yourself to others.

To control your internal monologue and resist the temptation to compare yourself to other people, speak or write mantras or affirmations. Stay focused on your own personal development and learning-path rather than getting immersed in what other people are doing or behaving jealously. You can redirect your efforts towards personal development rather than succumbing to the negative emotions of comparison and self-doubt by participating in conferences and seminars that offer opportunities to gain knowledge and skills. Upholding a positive mindset and overcoming external distractions are ongoing efforts that require self-awareness and conscious action.

I have been on YouTube for 10 years and have generated almost 30 million viewers, and if I am not careful, I can get caught in the trap of comparing myself to someone with higher views and subscribers. Despite my years of experience, I must remain aware of these triggers and make efforts to prevent sliding into unproductive routines. Keeping a positive outlook and pressing forward on your path to self-improvement, requires you to learn from others and concentrate on yourself without giving in to jealousy or other bad feelings. Always keep in mind that hard effort and devotion are the keys to success and that by recognizing and admiring the accomplishments of others, you might find inspiration to achieve greatness in your own life.

If you're in the process of building a substantial business with clear goals and a strong vision, it's essential to take action toward realizing your aspirations. However, it's crucial to understand that success doesn't happen overnight. It may appear as if someone is an overnight millionaire or they have achieved their wealth suddenly, but trust me, that's not the way it happens. There is much more to the story. Behind the scenes, there are years of dedication and hard work. Before notable achievements,

WHAT IF YOU FAIL?

there are often numerous setbacks, rejections, and a learning curve involved. It's a journey of trial and error, where refining strategies, scripts, and approaches is key. Just like the famous inventor, Thomas Edison, who faced numerous failures before inventing the light bulb, setbacks are a common part of the journey. Everyone experiences challenges and obstacles along the way, but perseverance and continuous improvement are vital for achieving great things.

I truly consider myself a success story because of my experience with rebuilding my life and business after bankruptcy. In the realm of real estate, my success blossomed from dealing with numerous foreclosures. Similarly, my journey as an author saw me achieving success despite facing rejections from publishers for books that never made it to print. I vividly recall sending out a children's book manuscript to over a hundred publishers, all of whom turned it down. This struggle is a stark contrast to the well-known author of the Harry Potter series, who famously received 33 rejections. Surprisingly, this setback turned into a triumph as self-publishing enabled me to earn more than I ever would have with a traditional publisher.

Failing versus Failure

Do you know that failing in an area is not the same as being a failure? Failing is a process of trial and error. It means you are discovering what works and what doesn't. Sure, at times it can be costly, however, failing allows us the grace to figure it out. Even after my bankruptcy, I was able to later build business credit to grow my business. Although it was a temporary setback, it was not a final or permanent closure to my being able to maintain financial independence.

Failure on the other hand is a permanent state. Failure is when you fall and decide to stay there and not try again. If you have failed in anything...keep reading. These simple yet important tips will help you to bounce back. I truly believe we have the power to control our destiny.

- Maintain a Positive Outlook: Don't dwell on the things you consider to be a failure. Instead, consistently remind yourself that everything is unfolding in your favor. When you maintain this perspective, there is no room for failure or negativity. Even situations that seem unfavorable or challenging may hold hidden opportunities beyond your current understanding. Whether you attribute these possibilities to a higher power, the universe, or simply the concept of a greater source, acknowledging that there are unknown variables at play can be empowering.

- See Beyond! Can you see a positive outlook for your future? Don't dwell on where you are in the moment. Your current state is only temporary. What happened yesterday has already passed on. What awaits you in your future is full of potential and unforeseen opportunities. Keep your eyes focused on the vision and believe that you can and will do it.

- Embrace Failing: Every setback is a stepping stone towards your eventual success. Redirect your focus towards positive outcomes and remain resilient in the face of adversity. Reflect on what led you to the moment, and trace your steps, adjusting the place where you missed your footing.

PICK A HORSE

Don't Let the Stress of Temporary Setback Overwhelm You

After years of experiencing million-dollar coaching profits, one year I missed the mark. It was the first occasion in over five years that I did not cross over a million dollars. Because I know that failing (or not reaching my goal) is not failure, the revelation did not evoke any sensation. My disposition remains consistent whether I am earning millions in my coaching business or not. It's all about having a steady and confident disposition because life is still good. The temporary setback allowed me to innovate. I shifted to writing more books and working on the next launch of my business. Today, I am securing corporate clients, traveling to international locations to host events, and partnering with other businesses that understand the importance of global expansion. Innovation—the ability to grow, adapt, and restructure is key. My next aspiration is to earn one hundred million dollars annually. That is a mark I have never reached but I know it's not difficult to attain.

In his article "Positive Intelligence," author Shawn Achor reminds us "It's important to remember that stress has an upside."[18] Making a list of your worries is his recommendation for when you feel overwhelmed or fixated on failures. Make a note of which ones you have some say over and which ones are out of your hands. Pick out one variable you have some influence over and devise a simple, actionable plan to lower it. You may gently guide your thoughts back to a more positive and productive state of mind.

Neurologist Judy Willis, MD, shares that "neuroimaging studies reveal...there are specific and reproducible patterns of changing neural activity and brain structures associated with stress."[19] According to her, when people are under a lot of pressure, scans show that the higher-order, reflective brain isn't working as well as the lower-order, reactive brain, which is responsible for controlling uncontrollable behaviors and emotions. What's more, she claims, is that as time goes on, the density and speed of the connections between neurons in the lower-order, emotion-driven reactive networks grow, while the corresponding connections in the higher-order, reflective brain shrink.

According to Willis' research, retraining your brain to associate success with positive emotions rather than negative ones is a more beneficial exercise than concentrating on potential negative outcomes. Her advice is to strive for something that will provide you with "frequent recognition feedback of incremental progress." Dopa-

PICK A HORSE

mine, which is released when these goals are reached, enhances motivation and persistence.

Innovation After Failing

"Amazon turns $2.7 Billion Loss in 2022 to a profit of $30 Billion in 2023."[20]

Amazon's CEO, Andy Jassy attributed the financial improvement to the reorganization of Amazon's U.S. fulfillment network along regional lines, a move Jassy said improved delivery times while also cutting costs. The reorganization, the company reported, allowed the company to deliver 4 billion units to U.S. customers within one day of ordering last year.

Amazon, one of today's biggest multinational companies, operated at a loss for nine years before achieving profitability. Consider the fact that Walt Disney filed for bankruptcy before successfully establishing Walt Disney and Disney World as the iconic entities we know today. Five years later, Disney created his most iconic character—Mickey Mouse. Abraham Lincoln was nearly fifty years old before making a significant impact, and Colonel Sanders, the founder of KFC, experienced multiple setbacks and didn't find success until his fifties.

These examples serve as a reminder that success doesn't always come early in life and neither does it come without hardships. If you have tried to attain personal freedom and it seems as if you are hitting a brick wall, don't worry, you are in good company. The winner's circle is filled with people who repeatedly faced loss. Personal achievements may take time to materialize, and milestones can be reached at different stages of one's journey. The difference is they didn't quit. I encourage you to stay committed, resilient, and persistent, regardless of age or past experiences.

A setback is just a temporary delay on the road to success when you're an entrepreneur. You can pick yourself up, dust yourself off, and try again after every obstacle you encounter. Keep in mind that even the most prosperous businesspeople in history had lots of setbacks on the way to becoming the most successful they could be. Acknowledge setbacks as opportunities for growth rather than focus on the setbacks themselves. Never give up on your dreams; they are worth fighting for. When you have a positive attitude and persevere through the trials, you can realize your business aspirations, no matter how difficult the journey may be.

Standing in front of the room of only six attendees, built a resilience in me that, today, allows me to be seen by

PICK A HORSE

millions weekly. There must be something inside you that declares where I am today is just a stepping stone to where I am going. This is not my final destination. Failing is *temporary*. It is not an end but a temporary pause in your journey. Keep moving forward, learning from each experience, and you will inevitably progress towards your goals.

Chapter Questions:

1. What lessons can I learn from my failures that can help me innovate and improve in the future?

2. How can I shift my mindset to see failure not as a roadblock but as a necessary part of the journey towards innovation?

3. In what ways can I leverage my past failures to inspire creative solutions and breakthrough ideas in my personal or professional life?

Chapter Review

- Facing rejection is a common experience for many successful individuals, especially those who aspire to become wealthy CEOs of organizations.

- It's about turning rejection into motivation, using it as a steppingstone towards growth and success.

- Personal development is key to surviving and thriving, especially when going through tough situations.

- The way you communicate with yourself plays a significant role in how you tackle challenges and build mental resilience.

- To control your internal monologue and resist the temptation to compare yourself to other people, speak or write mantras or affirmations.

- Failing is a process of trial and error. It means you are discovering what works and what doesn't. Failure on the other hand is a permanent state.

○ The winner's circle is filled with people who repeatedly faced loss. Personal achievements may take time to materialize and milestones can be reached at different stages of one's journey.

CHAPTER TEN

Don't Chase It! Get in the Flow of Wealth

*M*OM, *I MADE it!* The NBA draft is a pivotal moment, not just for the young athletes whose names might be called, but equally for their families who have supported them throughout their journey. It's a spectacle that combines hope, anxiety, and the culmination of years of hard work and dedication. For the mothers of these athletes, it's a particularly profound experience. They sit in the glare of the national spotlight. Often, these women have nurtured their sons' talents, driven them to countless practices and games, and provided emotional support through every high and low.

For the players, being drafted is not just about the sport; it's a life-changing event that offers financial rewards which, until draft day, might have seemed like a distant dream. The transition from college or amateur basketball to the NBA is monumental, marked by not just an increase in the level of play, but by the new responsibilities and pressures that come with being a professional athlete. It's a moment of immense transformation, where dreams are actualized and the groundwork for a career in the NBA is laid.

Yet, amidst the fanfare of the draft, the true heart of the moment lies in the personal stories of these young men and their families. It's about the daily sacrifices made, the obstacles overcome, and the unwavering belief in their potential. For the mothers watching, it's a validation of their faith and support, a shared achievement that transcends the sport itself. The NBA draft is more than just an event; it's a celebration of talent, hard work, and the deep familial bonds that have helped shape the next generation of basketball stars.

I can only imagine the nervousness intertwined with excitement that is felt when these young players are drafted by professional teams that offer them salaries beyond their wildest dreams. When you listen to their acceptance speeches, they often give acknowledgement to their support team and coaches. So often you hear a tearful thank you to their mother—the person that has been consistent in their lives.

When my real estate income became more consistent, and my net worth had increased substantially, I couldn't wait to let my parents know I did it! I had achieved the American dream. I wanted them to be proud of what I had accomplished and how hard I had worked. More than anything, I wanted my mom to see that I was not the same hopeless pregnant woman, just years prior, who needed to move into her basement. To prove I had made it, I showered her with gifts, from name-brand designer handbags to luxury cars. To my surprise, the material wealth didn't equate to what they believed was success was. Seeking validation and approval, no matter what I earned, was something that I had to work through. Whether they considered what I did as "real work" or not was not my issue—it was theirs. I knew that I had found my purpose, and I had to be willing to pursue it even if that meant not meeting their approval.

That was a hard truth I had to learn to accept. I know that my parents have always loved me, but one day I had to come to terms with my expectations of them. We had different definitions of success and I had to be okay with that. We couldn't change each other's opinions on the matter. I am not saying it's easy to do, especially when the people you want to celebrate with you the most, don't. However, it also doesn't mean they don't care about you. It means that you need to grow to a place where what matters most is how you see yourself. Sure, we want the support of the ones that we love and trust, but will you be able to move past their limited perceptions and ideas?

It was through my quiet moments of introspection and personal development that I began to understand the significance of focusing on self-improvement and finding inner peace. By immersing myself in valuable teachings about self-worth, I underwent a transformation in my perception of wealth and success. As I reflect on my journey, I've come to realize that the pursuit of external validation and the constant need to impress others, particularly through material success, only leads to emptiness. I now see money as a reflection of the value I offer to the world rather than a means to seek validation from others. We shouldn't try to buy anyone's love. I will take it a bit further and say, that seeking validation from others causes you to feel down about yourself and creates an energy that constricts your money flow.

Money is Energy

While I juggle the roles of a parent, spouse, and business owner, I've grasped the concept that financial stability is crucial, but true wealth encompasses far more than just monetary riches. It's about cultivating a sense of fulfillment that transcends the need for external approval or validation. Therefore, I cannot end this book without talking about the topic of the energy of money. Many people don't understand what it takes to grow wealth and how the more you worry about money, the less you have of it. If you want your wealth to grow over time, you must learn to be comfortable with money. Money is energy. This means if you are stressed about it, you can't create it. To grow your money, you must keep an optimistic and emotionally high-frequency attitude about your life. Money is a positive force that responds positively to value creation.

When you dwell on emotions like vengeance, sadness, depression, debt, worry, and overwhelm, your financial situation is likely to suffer because money operates on an energetic and frequency level. Conversely, by cultivating happiness, optimism, and a mindset focused on adding value to others and being a positive role model, you can elevate your financial prospects.

Your Money Flow

When the environment is set for money, it will flow. Since money is energy and currency, it isn't just about the cash in your wallet or the numbers in your bank account. It's about the emotions, beliefs, and energy that come along with it. It's like a flowing river, always moving and changing. Bank balances, stock values, and real estate numbers can go up and down. When you understand this, you don't attach any emotion to it. True wealth isn't just about how much money you have; it's about how you see and feel about your financial situation. Instead of stressing over the ups and downs, focus on creating value for others. By shifting your mindset to one of abundance and positivity, you can attract more wealth and success into your life.

To create a healthy relationship with money, it's essential to recognize and address any negative beliefs or emotions you may have toward it. This should include being honest about your previous financial experiences, identifying your values and priorities, and changing your thinking to see money as a tool for attaining your life of freedom. We all have a money story. The difference between those that become wealthy and those that don't is what emotions are tied to the story.

PICK A HORSE

Did you lose a large sum of money and now you are afraid to take the risk again?

Did you grow up not having enough money, and now you hold tight to everything you get?

Did your parents constantly tell you they couldn't afford something?

Whatever your money story is, it's important that you release any emotion surrounding it. You must release the negative emotions attached to that story or you'll never attract what you want. I often find that people who talk about wanting money, without taking action, are blocked by their limiting beliefs. These money blockages prevent them from ever achieving financial success. No matter how big you dream, if you don't address these areas, you will not be able to attain your unlimited money flow. Financial freedom is not just about having a pile of cash; it's about the positive impact it can have. Imagine the good you can do with financial abundance—helping others, supporting causes you care about, and making the world a better place. It's not about greed; it's about using your resources for good.

Everything is Working Out for You

Have you heard of the idea that everything is always working out for you? It's a powerful mindset that can transform how you approach challenges. When you believe that things are falling into place, you feel empowered to tackle anything that comes your way. This positive outlook, popularized by Abraham Hicks, can bring a sense of peace and resilience, even in tough times. Embracing this mantra opens up a world of possibilities and helps you see obstacles as opportunities for growth. When you accept that everything in your life is aligning for your good – you can eliminate worry, anxiety, fear, doubt, and uncertainty. By adopting this perspective, you can face problems with assurance, understanding that each experience, regardless of its nature, is leading you towards personal development and reward. Surrendering to life's flow allows you to access a realm of possibilities and opportunities often hidden by fear and doubt.

Exude Gratitude

Staying in a place of gratitude is a foundational principle to attain wealth and keeps you in your money flow. We live in a society where complaining is often accepted and tolerated. Quite honestly, we live in an ungrateful world. I don't think we are grateful enough for the things we "get to do" vs "have to do." Let me explain what I mean. Instead of viewing everything you do as a burdensome task, reframe your thinking and see the opportunity as a blessing instead of a burden. Shift your perspective. For example, rather than saying "I have to take my kids to school," you can adopt a mindset of gratitude by saying "I get to take my kids to school," appreciating the moments and experiences that come with it. By embracing these opportunities and reframing them positively, you can cultivate a mindset of growth and fulfillment in various aspects of your life. And for me, I'll be honest, it is amazing.

This mindset allows you to see how much control you do have. I remember working a job and just dropping my kids off and running and rushing them to quickly exit the car because I was late for work. Now I get to take my time. I am available to attend their school events and field trips. I have the opportunity to volunteer and be present in my kids' lives. Think about how you can apply this gratitude principle to your life. What if instead of complaining about paying bills you say, "I get to pay my bill." How about applying this to working out? The next time you think about it, don't dread it. Instead, say, I get to run, I get to walk, I get to exercise. This should be applied to every area of your life.

Shhhh! There's Too Much Noise

Quieting the noise around us also creates our money flow. I find it difficult to operate at my highest self when I am surrounded by noise. I don't mean actual noise, I mean the noise of negative news, negative people, and constant competition. We live in a time where entrepreneurs are constantly posting their incomes and their lavish lifestyles. Although I am not totally against showcasing what you have achieved from a branding or marketing perspective, there is a way to tastefully do it. If you have watched my YouTube page, you may have heard me often mention I am a millionaire. This isn't from a place of bragging or to make you feel like you aren't enough because you are. I speak on these things from a place of building wealth and motivating you to strive for this as well. I want you to see the success of my journey to give you hope that it is possible for you. I do this to bring credibility to my brand. However, please understand these

PICK A HORSE

things are all material, and I don't place my value in them. This is one reason why I have consciously limited my time on social media. It often serves as a breeding ground for such comparison and competition.

In recent times, I have made the decision to step away from certain mastermind groups because I found that they brought out a level of unhealthy competition that made me uncomfortable. Picture being in a room full of ambitious individuals all trying to outshine one another, constantly boasting about their financial successes. It became a bit like a contest of who could one-up the other the most. Someone would say they made $2 million in a year, only for another member to claim they earned that in a month, and another person topping that by saying they made it in a week. It honestly felt quite awkward to witness. This kind of environment not only encourages dishonesty but also reveals the true nature of individuals. The focus on comparing and competing to see who can amass more wealth, clients, properties, or possessions ultimately felt draining and unsatisfying, leaving me feeling disheartened. I came to the realization that constantly comparing myself to others and getting caught up in fierce competition was not doing me any favors, so I decided to step away from those situations.

It's important to tune out any negative voices and focus on your own path. Avoid falling into the trap of constantly comparing yourself to others and getting caught up in competition. While I have always looked up to successful mentors and valued their guidance, I never wanted to copy them or get into a race of "one-upmanship." The unhealthy cycle of comparing achievements, chasing material possessions, and striving to be the best in terms of financial success only led to feeling dissatisfied and unfulfilled. Find fulfillment in your own accomplishments and define success on your own terms rather than trying to compete with others. Stay true to yourself, focus on your journey, and don't let the pressures of comparison and competition steer you off course.

Do you remember the classic tale of the hare and the tortoise? The tortoise's steady pace won the race. It's not always about speed; it's about embracing the journey and the process in your business endeavors. Whether you're aiming to get fit or shed some pounds, the secret ingredient is consistency. Hit the gym regularly, maintain a healthy diet, and stay patient—results take time. Falling in love with the process is where the magic truly happens.

In the world of entrepreneurship, self-discipline, motivation, and resilience are your best friends. Challenges will come your way, but it's how you bounce back that counts. Stay strong, learn from setbacks, and keep pushing forward. Breaking down your goals and crafting a solid strategy will pave the way for your success. Transitioning from a regular job to a thriving business bringing in seven figures is possible with the right mindset and determination. Your journey has brought you to where you are today, and every experience along the way has shaped you.

Take a moment to reflect on what you've learned while working with others. Think about the unique gifts, talents, and personalities you've encountered. What valuable lessons have stood out to you? Are there areas where you've noticed a company could improve? Life is full of conversations that may be tough or awkward. Whether it's delivering difficult news, managing performance issues, or handling challenging clients, these moments are part of growth. They say that success lies in the willingness to have those uncomfortable conversations. In *Crucial Conversations: Tools for Talking When Stakes are High* by Joseph Greeny, the importance of facing such situations head-on is emphasized.

Don't allow the outside world to affect your inner peace. Get in alignment with your money creativity flow and allow your world to change. Once I released the weight of the opinions of others and became laser-focused, things began to rapidly increase for me. I didn't always understand the importance and energy of money, but once I did, it became a life principle I applied. When my money flow changes, I quickly begin to evaluate my thoughts, my environment, and my actions. We are in control of how much money is attracted to us. If you are not where you want to be today, go ahead and make the pivot.

Affirmations:

1. Everything is always working out for me, even when I can't see it.

2. I trust in the process of life and know that everything is unfolding perfectly for me.

3. I attract positive outcomes effortlessly because everything is always working out for me.

4. Challenges are just opportunities in disguise, and everything is always working out for me.

5. I am a magnet for miracles because everything is always working out for me.

6. The universe conspires in my favor, and everything is always working out for me.

7. I release all worries and fears because everything is always working out for me.

8. Every setback is a setup for a comeback because everything is always working out for me.

9. I am deserving of all good things because everything is always working out for me.

10. I am grateful for the blessings coming my way because everything is always working out for me.

11. Abundance flows to me effortlessly because everything is always working out for me.

12. I radiate positivity and attract success because everything is always working out for me.

13. I am a powerful creator, and everything is always working out for me.

14. I let go of control and surrender to the flow of life because everything is always working out for me.

15. I am open to receiving all the good that the universe has in store for me because everything is always working out for me.

16. I am aligned with the energy of abundance, and everything is always working out for me.

17. I trust in divine timing and know that everything is always working out for me.

18. My path is unfolding perfectly, and everything is always working out for me.

19. I am a magnet for positive opportunities because everything is always working out for me.

20. I am blessed beyond measure because everything is always working out for me.

21. I am worthy of love, success, and happiness because everything is always working out for me.

22. I am the creator of my reality, and everything is always working out for me.

23. I embrace uncertainty knowing that everything is always working out for me.

PICK A HORSE

24. I am guided and supported by the universe because everything is always working out for me.

25. I am a beacon of light attracting all that is good because everything is always working out for me.

Chapter Review

○ See money as a reflection of the value you offer to the world rather than a means to seek validation from others.

○ To create a healthy relationship with money, it's essential to recognize and address any negative beliefs or emotions you may have toward it.

○ When you accept that everything in your life is aligning for your good – you can eliminate worry, anxiety, fear, doubt, and uncertainty.

○ It's important to tune out any negative voices and focus on your own path. Avoid falling into the trap of constantly comparing yourself to others and getting caught up in competition.

○ Find fulfillment in your own accomplishments and define success on your own terms rather than trying to compete with others.

CHAPTER ELEVEN

Embrace the Process and Ride It!

One day while accompanying one of my artists to a radio interview, we found ourselves in a moment of reflection amidst the hum of the elevator. My artist, caught in a moment of aspiration, spoke aloud about his future, dreaming of the day when he would "make it big" and achieve significant fame. It was a pivotal moment, one that required clarity and perspective. I felt compelled to share with him a truth that I had come to realize over my years in business. I gently explained that the journey he was on, at that very moment, was the essence of 'making it.' The real achievement lay in the present—in every radio interview attended, every song written, every beat crafted, and every collaboration with a producer. I stressed that the value of his work and his art did not

EMBRACE THE PROCESS AND RIDE IT!

hinge on future milestones like chart rankings or awards ceremonies. I wanted him to understand that every step of his artistic journey, every day of his life was significant.

"This is it," I told him. "This is the realization of what truly defines what making it in the music industry really is, it's not about the accolades that may come later. It's not simply about rushing to the finish line; it's about embracing the journey itself." Achieving success is not marked by reaching a certain number of followers. The numbers don't mark the culmination of your efforts. Whether you're like my artist, heading to a radio interview, crafting a song, or collaborating with a producer, these moments are integral parts of the journey. These are the steps towards a grand finale.

Life isn't punctuated by dramatic milestones as many would imagine. What I hope you take away from this book is a deeper understanding that choosing your path, much like selecting a horse in a race, is only the beginning. I emphasized to him that the essence of success wasn't in some distant future event but in the passion and effort he put into his work every single day. The moment I realized I had become a millionaire, wasn't accompanied by fanfare. Waiting on the receipt of awards, grand acknowledgments or celebratory milestones shouldn't be the focus. The daily grind, be it responding to a client's email, hosting a webinar, creating content for YouTube, penning down thoughts for a book, coaching clients, or buying properties—these are the actions that should define the essence of success. This realization is crucial: the reality of success lies in the process, in the everyday efforts and achievements that build upon each other. Looking for a defining moment of arrival or an ultimate accolade misses the point entirely. The real achievement is in the doing, in the love and passion you pour into your work every day.

Looking Back at the Shore

A mentor once taught me an essential part of truly relishing life, which he termed "looking back at the shore." He explained in our life we are between two shores. The one behind us and the one in front of us. Often, we find ourselves in the thick of our journey, metaphorically swimming from one shore to another in pursuit of our life's goals. This phase, which I like to call being 'in the process,' can feel akin to being adrift in the of the sea—where the origin and destination shores are out of sight, leaving us with a sense of isolation in the vast ocean. This analogy beautifully illustrates the importance of occasionally pausing to reflect on the progress we've made. It's not just about reaching the next milestone but also about appreciating the journey thus far. Acknowledging how much ground you've covered should bring you a sense of joy and accomplishment. Even when the "other shore" or our ultimate goal seems out of reach, recognizing the distance you've traveled, the hurdles you've overcome, and the achievements along the way can be incredibly uplifting.

Reflecting on how far you've come, much like looking back at the shore when swimming across the ocean, offers a more fulfilling sense of accomplishment than any award or material milestone could. It reminds me of my ambitious goal of reaching more subscribers on my YouTube page. I escalated from 5,000 subscribers to 50,000, 100,000, and eventually over 300,000. Initially, I believed each milestone would bring an overwhelming sense of accomplishment. Surprisingly, the emotional impact was not as profound as I anticipated, even when reaching 100,000 subscribers. Each major milestone felt no different from the earlier one.

The arrival of the YouTube Silver Play Button, despite its significance, did not bring the sense of fulfillment I had imagined. I am not saying that it wasn't a momentous occasion that should not have been celebrated. I did my share of holding it in my hands, capturing that moment

PICK A HORSE

for my audience; it was perfect for content creation and marketing. These days, it probably means more to my subscribers because it's a form of recognition and credibility, tangible proof of my channel's growth and influence. But I have to admit, once the excitement wore off, it became another accessory for my filming setup.

After having this transformation in my thinking, I gave myself permission to remove the pressure to live up to someone else's standards. When I changed my focus, I became passionate about the process we put into place to deliver content that keeps people watching and subscribing to my channel. My team and I find more reward in diving into research, seeking topics that resonate with our audience, and delivering valuable and engaging content. This commitment to bringing value to my viewers has become my source of joy and fulfillment. Embracing and enjoying the creative process, rather than fixating on awards or subscriber counts, has become my true measure of success and dedication poured into every video.

Life, especially when dedicated to fulfilling one's purpose and dreams, is continuous. Authentic satisfaction should be found in the work itself and the value you bring to others. Each day is a testament to living your truth. While embarking on your path, whether as a rapper heading to a radio interview or as a real estate millionaire, it's crucial to understand that there isn't a singular, defining moment that solidifies your status in your field. It's not standing on the stage at the Grammys nor is it hitting a specific number of properties owned, or reaching a milestone valuation that truly makes you who you are. These high points, these moments of recognition and celebration, are merely the byproducts of the relentless, day-in and day-out grind that characterizes the essence of success. It's the commitment to the process, the dedication to the craft, that truly matters.

One day you will achieve your pinnacle. Whether it's earning a million dollars, or acquiring that dream mansion or luxury car, these milestones, though significant, shouldn't change the focus of your pursuit. They are checkpoints, not endpoints. A million dollars in the bank or the keys to a Lamborghini—while impressive, are just objects and numbers. They don't epitomize it; rather, they are evidence of the journey undertaken to reach them.

Are You Ready to Ride Your Horse?

This is the point of the book where I challenge you to take everything you have read so far and make your decision on what you want for your life. If you are stuck

PICK A HORSE

between indecision and fear, I want to push you to get out of your head and go for what you know you deserve. Admittedly, it took me far too long to trust myself again, so I know what this feels like. Ultimately, you will find yourself frustrated and overwhelmed with your life. This is because there is an internal struggle about where you are today. Once I made the decision to leave my full-time job, I embarked on the journey of transitioning into full-time entrepreneurship. I set a goal of six months before taking the leap and began the countdown. With each passing day, from five months, to four, to three, I ticked off the milestones. This countdown symbolized my path to independence and self-reliance, no longer dependent on a steady paycheck from my previous job.

Have you selected your "bet-on-me" date? If not do that now! When are you going to take the leap and give life all you've got? If I could leave you with lasting wisdom, it would be this. Embrace every step, every challenge, and every small victory along the way. Find fulfillment in the continuous pursuit of excellence, not just in the moments of recognition. And live your life with purpose and focused intentions. Whatever you do, don't quit! Entrepreneurs come from all walks of life—whether extroverted, introverted, neurodiverse, or from any underrepresented community. Cultivate resilience and maintain a positive inner dialogue. Becoming an entrepreneur demands

EMBRACE THE PROCESS AND RIDE IT!

more than just raw talent or intelligence—it requires dedication and unwavering perseverance.

As you have reached the conclusion of this book, I hope you have found inspiration and valuable insights throughout. Now, it's time for action. Take a moment to reflect on the chapters, internalize the lessons, and implement them in your own life. My wish is to one day delve into the pages of your success story. Revisit the contents of this book, identify the areas that require your immediate focus, and take the necessary steps toward your goals.

PICK A HORSE

Learning Never Stops

SCAN HERE

Coaching & Mentorship

NoelleRandall.com/Mentorship

References

1. Statista, "Wealth distribution in the United States in the third quarter of 2023", December 2023 (https://www.statista.com/statistics/203961/wealth-distribution-for-the-us/) Accessed April 7, 2024
2. Julia Carrie Wong, "Uber CEO Travis Kalanick caught on video arguing with driver about fares", The Guardian, March 1st, 2017 (https://www.theguardian.com/technology/2017/feb/28/uber-ceo-travis-kalanick-driver-argument-video-fare-prices) Accessed February 16, 2024
3. Kate Conger, "Uber Founder Travis Kalanick Leaves Board, Severing Last Tie", New York Times, December 24th, 2019 (https://www.nytimes.com/2019/12/24/technology/uber-travis-kalanick.html#:~:text=Investors%20forced%20Mr) Accessed February 16, 2024
4. Victoria Lewis, "Mental Health: The Silent Battle of 72% of Startup Founders", December 29th, 2023 (https://www.victorialewis.co.uk/post/

founder-mental-health?utm_campaign=dd1c551a-d5ce-404b-8284-9b44dc14444b&utm_source=so&utm_medium=mail) Accessed February 17, 2024
5. Kathleen Elkins, "Rich People Exercise Every Day", Business Insider, April 5th, 2016 (https://www.businessinsider.com/rich-people-exercise-every-day-2016-4#:~:text=In%20his%20research%2C%20he%20noticed,Habits%2C%20Change%20Your%20Life.%22) Accessed February 17, 2024
6. Christopher Murray, "The Largest Banks in the U.S.", MarketWatch, April 5th, 2024 (https://www.marketwatch.com/guides/banking/largest-banks-in-the-us/) Accessed February 17, 2024
7. Elena Lytkina Botelho, Kim Rosenkoetter Powell, Stephen Kincaid, and Dina Wang. "What Sets Successful CEO's Apart", Harvard Business Review, May 2017 https://hbr.org/2017/05/what-sets-successful-ceos-apart Accessed March 3, 2024
8. Amy Fisken, "The road to riches: the importance of decisiveness according to Napoleon Hill", July 2019, (https://www.penguin.co.uk/articles/2019/07/road-to-riches-decisiveness-napoleon-hill) Accessed April 7, 2024
9. Frank Graff, "How Many Decisions Do We Make In One Day?", PBS, August 13th 2021 (https://www.

REFERENCES

pbsnc.org/blogs/science/how-many-decisions-do-we-make-in-one-day/#:~:text=Thousands%20of%20choices%20every%20day&text=And%20as%20your%20level%20of,are%20both%20good%20and%20bad) Accessed February 21, 2024

10. Melanie Perkins, "How Canva's Melanie Perkins Learned to Pitch Persuasively After More Than 100 Rejections", Inc, September 27th, 2021 (https://www.inc.com/carmine-gallo/how-canvas-melanie-perkins-learned-to-pitch-persuasively-after-more-than-100-rejections.html) Accessed February 15, 2024

11. Alex Konrad, "Canva Uncovered: How A Young Australian Kitesurfer Built A $3.2 Billion (Profitable!) Startup Phenom", Forbes, December 11th, 2019 (https://www.forbes.com/sites/alexkonrad/2019/12/11/inside-canva-profitable-3-billion-startup-phenom/?sh=4ea4f75f4a51) Accessed February 15, 2024

12. Apollo Technical, "20 ENTREPRENEUR STATISTICS YOU NEED TO KNOW (2023)", September 22nd, 2023 (https://www.apollotechnical.com/entrepreneur-statistics/#:~:text=According%20to%20Guidant%20Financial%2C%20about%2030%25%20of%20entrepreneurs%20only%20finish,be%20very%20important%20for%20entrepreneurship) Accessed February 24, 2024

13. Branson, R. 2014. March 27. https://twitter.com/richardbranson/status/449220072176107520?lang=en Accessed February 24, 2024
14. Michelle Hansen, "How to Build a Brand Culture", Formulate, (does not specify date) (https://www.formulates.io/post/build-a-winning-brand-culture#:~:text=Brand%20Culture%20is%20the%20system,the%20values%20inside%20the%20company) Accessed February 24, 2024
15. Rabbi Avi S. Olitzky, "We're all in the same boat: What a 1,500 year old parable can teach us about this moment", Minnesota Reformer, August 7th, 2020 (https://minnesotareformer.com/2020/08/07/were-all-in-the-same-boat-what-a-1500-year-old-parable-can-teach-us-about-this-moment/) Accessed February 27, 2024
16. Amy Dickey, "5 Quotes From Billionaire Mark Cuban That Will Inspire You To Work Your Ass Off", Elite Daily, September 9th, 2014 (https://www.elitedaily.com/life/motivation/quotes-from-billionaire-mark-cuban/727103) Accessed February 27, 2024
17. Bailey Nelson, "Great Leaders Have These Leadership Skills in Common", Gallup CliftonStrengths, Updated May 10, 2023 https://www.gallup.com/cliftonstrengths/en/357983/great-leaders-behaviors-common.

REFERENCES

aspx#:~:text=Great%20leaders%20know%20that%20development,on%20growing%20their%20leadership%20qualities. Accessed February 28, 2024

18. Shawn Achor, "Positive Intelligence", Harvard Business Review, January - February 2012 (https://hbr.org/2012/01/positive-intelligence) Accessed February 29, 2024

19. Zadra Rose Ibañez, "What Happens When You Fail", Institute For Educational Advancement, April 10th, 2018 (https://educationaladvancement.org/blog-rewire-your-brain-for-success-when-you-fail/) Accessed February 29, 2024

20. Jim Millot, "Amazon Turns $2.7 Billion Loss in 2022 to a Profit of $30 Billion in 2023", Publishers Weekly, February 2nd, 2024 (https://www.publishersweekly.com/pw/by-topic/industry-news/financial-reporting/article/94240-amazon-turns-2-7-billion-loss-in-2022-to-a-profit-of-30-billion-in-2023.html#:~:text=News%20%3E%20Financial%20Reporting-,Amazon%20Turns%20%242.7%20Billion%20Loss%20in%202022%20to,of%20%2430%20Billion%20in%202023&text=Cost%20cuts%20and%20a%20record,tech%20giant%20reported%20Thursday%20afternoon.) Accessed February 29, 2024

Acknowledgments

THIS BOOK EMERGES from my compelling life's story, intricately woven through lessons learned from my teachers, mentors, and family. I share my wealth of experiences, which have profoundly shaped my life, to encourage you to step out into your purpose. I consider it the highest form of praise whenever someone says I've inspired or motivated them, as I am genuinely a reflection of all that I have learnt from others. It would be remiss of me not to acknowledge those individuals who have played a pivotal role in my growth.

My gratitude extends deeply to my family—my steadfast support system through my darkest moments. A heartfelt thank you to my mother, father, brother, and sister for their unwavering love and belief in me.

To my incredible husband. You have been my rock, my confidant, and my greatest advocate through it all. Your kindness, strength, and gentle spirit are unparalleled, and I am deeply thankful for your presence in my life. You are truly remarkable in every sense.

To my seven children—Adia, Nya, Kamryn, Bryce, Milan, Gabby, and Gavin—you have been my ultimate source of inspiration. Each one of you has taught me invaluable lessons about acceptance, unconditional love, and striving to be the best version of oneself. The insights I have gained from you are immeasurable.

Lastly, to those who have played a significant role in my personal and professional growth: Eckhart Tolle, Napoleon Hill, Robert Allen, Nate Woodbury, Russell Brunson, and Ken Van Liew. Thank you.

About the Author

NOELLE RANDALL IS a successful real estate entrepreneur, renowned author, mentor, speaker, and influencer. The story of her entrepreneurial journey and experiences gained along the way serves as the backbone that allows her to reach and inspire so many through her videos, books, courses, mentorship, and more. As a passionate believer that anyone can turn their dreams into reality with the right tools, knowledge, and resources, Noelle has provided these to the world through her ever-expanding social media presence with a heavy focus on her constantly growing YouTube subscriber base. She has taken her message further by putting knowledge in the hands of passionate entrepreneurs seeking success with free access to her books, through special virtual and live events, and through her carefully created courses and mentorship programs. From starting any business to building a real estate empire or rental car fleet and beyond, Noelle has helped hundreds through her coaching programs and thousands through her YouTube videos.

As CEO of NuuRez, Noelle has taken her knowledge of real estate investing and short-term rentals to create one of the fastest crowd-funded real estate investment groups. By utilizing the same methods that she teaches in her courses, NuuRez has created a growing portfolio of luxury properties across several states that attract renters through Airbnb, VRBO, and more while increasing in profits year over year.

Noelle's belief that knowledge should be accessible to all, further drove her to create the Marley Simms Foundation, a public non-profit organization dedicated to children's literacy and promoting diversity by providing access to a variety of authors and fostering the discussion of a wide range of topics.

Most recently, Noelle has followed her love of music to create a unique record label that will help bands of all genres gain the knowledge to succeed and the exposure to achieve their dreams! This revolutionary new label aims to become the go-to label for up-and-coming artists across the country.

ABOUT THE AUTHOR

Noelle earned her Bachelor's degree from the University of Connecticut in Urban Planning. She has a Master's degree in Economic Development from Penn State and a Master's in Business Administration (MBA) from Baylor University.

Stay Connected

Website: https://noellerandall.com

Noelle Randall Podcast: https://podcasts.apple.com/us/podcast/noelle-randall-podcast/id1519093419

Youtube.com/noellerandall1

Instagram.com/noellerandallcoaching

Facebook.com/noellerandallcoaching

TikTok.com/noellerandallcoaching

Pinterest.com/noellerandall

Twitter.com/noelle_randall

Other books by Noelle

Real Estate Millionaire Secrets: The Real Beginner's Guide to Real Estate

Millionaire Business Secrets: The Real Beginner's Guide to Starting a Business

BNB Millionaire Secrets: The Real Blueprint to Short-term Rental Success

Turo Millionaire Secrets: Turning Business Credit and Cars into a Million-Dollar Business

Made in the USA
Middletown, DE
15 September 2025